MINDFUL
SELF-
COMPASSION

MINDFUL
Self-
Compassion

Practical Strategies to Cultivate
Self-Awareness and Nurture
Emotional Well-Being

TIFFANY SHELTON MARIOLLE, PHD

ROCKRIDGE
PRESS

For general information on our other products and services or to obtain technical support, please contact our Customer Care Department within the United States at (866) 744-2665, or outside the United States at (510) 253-0500.

Rockridge Press publishes its books in a variety of electronic and print formats. Some content that appears in print may not be available in electronic books, and vice versa.

TRADEMARKS: Rockridge Press and the Rockridge Press logo are trademarks or registered trademarks of Callisto Media Inc. and/or its affiliates, in the United States and other countries, and may not be used without written permission. All other trademarks are the property of their respective owners. Rockridge Press is not associated with any product or vendor mentioned in this book.

Interior and Cover Designer: Jami Spittler   Editor: Lori Tenny
Art Producer: Sue Bischofberger   Production Editor: Jenna Dutton.

Illustrations © Creative Market and Design Cuts

ISBN: Print 978-1-64739-619-0 | eBook 978-1-64739-620-6

R0

I dedicate this book to
my loving husband, Jean Victor,
and my baby girl, Layla.

Contents

Introduction

Sometimes it feels impossible to silence our inner critic and all the negativity that may accompany it: perfectionism, judgmental thoughts, insecurity, and anxiety. But you *can* stop the cycle of self-criticism by replacing it with self-compassion. When we foster self-compassion, we gain the ability to love ourselves even in the face of our failures, flaws, and inadequacies. With self-compassion, you're able to be warm and kind toward yourself during your most painful moments.

As a psychologist, I've helped many clients cultivate healing self-compassion to combat depression, low self-esteem, and difficult emotional experiences such as guilt and shame. More importantly, I've seen self-compassion help many people live more joyful, loving, and resilient lives.

For a variety of reasons, it's not always easy to show compassion to ourselves. In this book, you'll learn how self-compassion can be achieved using the practice of *mindfulness*, focusing on the present moment, so you can let go of distractions, understand where negativity is coming from, and tune in to the most important times to be compassionate with yourself. This mindful approach to self-compassion can help you overcome stress, difficult emotions, low self-worth, and self-criticism. It can transform the way you see yourself and life's challenges and empower you to persevere while loving yourself along the way.

In reading *Mindful Self-Compassion*, you'll not only come to understand the importance of self-kindness and how it can change your life, you'll learn more than fifty different mindfulness-based techniques and exercises to help you instill self-compassion in your life. In chapter 1, we'll take a deeper dive into the meaning of self-compassion and how mindfulness can bring you to it. The subsequent chapters will each focus on a different aspect of your well-being. We'll discuss mindful strategies that will help with your thoughts (chapter 2), your emotions (chapter 3), your body (chapter 4), and your everyday habits (chapter 5). This holistic approach to cultivating self-compassion will equip you with strategies and practical tools for mind, body, and spirit, so you can make self-compassion part of your daily lifestyle.

Throughout this book, you'll find helpful journal prompts intended to give you an opportunity to reflect on your journey toward a more compassionate self. I highly encourage you to develop a journaling practice, if you do not already have one, as keeping a journal will help you add personal meaning to your self-love journey.

Congratulations on taking this huge step toward a more fulfilling, self-compassionate life. I'm certain of the power that mindful self-compassion has to change your life for the better—not just because I've seen it in my patients, but because I've experienced it myself. As a type A personality and a recovering perfectionist, I've found that cultivating mindful self-compassion gives me the freedom to love myself and my life, regardless of my accomplishments or life stressors. My goal is to offer you the same transformation that I've seen not only in my patients' lives but also in my own. I am so happy that you have decided to embark on this journey. I wish you joy as you bring yourself warmth, kindness, compassion, and love—mindfully.

Most unhappy people need to learn just one lesson: how to see themselves through the lens of genuine compassion and treat themselves accordingly.

—MARTHA BECK

Chapter 1

THE BASICS

Introduction

Most of us wouldn't think of kicking a friend while they're down or criticizing a loved one who comes to us for help and support. And yet, we seem to find it easy to be critical, unkind, and even cruel to ourselves. We don't grant ourselves the compassion that we extend to others.

How can we break our bad habits and put an end to our poor self-treatment, when most of the time we don't know we're doing it?

The answer is *mindfulness*. By attending to the present moment, by becoming mindful of how we react to life's challenges and obstacles, we're able to catch ourselves in the act of unhealthy self-talk and replace it with a voice of love, kindness, and encouragement. Practicing mindfulness is the means by which we develop *self-compassion*, the capacity to love ourselves unconditionally.

In this chapter, we're going to take a closer look at the nature of mindful self-compassion and how this spiritual superpower can improve the quality of your life. You'll learn six important characteristics of self-compassion that you will cultivate in yourself. You'll review the basic tenets of mindfulness, which will help you understand the exercises in the following chapters. Lastly, this chapter will offer best practices and advice on how to use this book to cultivate a life full of joy, self-love, and fulfillment.

The Superpower of Self-Compassion

You're worried about performing well at work or stressing over a mounting to-do list that feels impossible to complete. You spend hours on social media, feeling bad because everyone else's lives seem so much better than yours. You don't go after a job that you want because you're sure you're not good enough. Sometimes it seems impossible to avoid the pressures in our lives. But the truth is, you don't have to avoid them. You can change the way you respond to them instead and, in doing so, achieve a joyful, more satisfying life.

You can respond with the superpower of self-compassion, an antidote to modern life stressors such as pressures to be perfect, fit an ideal body type, or work yourself into the ground. Research on self-compassion has documented its ability to reduce levels of anxiety and depression, increase psychological flexibility and happiness, and improve physical health. Mindful self-compassion gives us the tools to persevere through stress, to cope with negative emotions, and to navigate difficult life events gracefully, all while loving ourselves in the process. Mindful self-compassion is the hidden superpower you didn't know you had, and it's time to activate it.

What Is Self-Compassion?

There are many ways to think about this superpower of yours. Psychologist Kristin Neff, who co-developed the Mindful Self-Compassion program with psychologist Christopher Germer, defines it as having three components: *mindfulness* (which she describes as observing our thoughts and feelings without judgment), *common humanity* (acknowledging that our personal flaws are part of the shared human condition), and *self-kindness*. Buddhist spiritual traditions discuss self-compassion as a form of loving-kindness for all beings, including oneself. Brené Brown, a

University of Houston professor who studies courage, vulnerability, shame, and empathy, describes self-compassion as a way to connect with our authentic selves (our true and pure identity, beyond our thoughts and defenses) and in the process become resilient to shame. Paul Gilbert, founder of the Compassionate Mind Foundation and creator of compassion-focused therapy (CFT), believes that self-compassion is the key to relieving intrusive feelings and shame.

That's a lot! But we can boil those overlapping descriptions down to this: Self-compassion is the ability to mindfully honor one's true self in totality, no matter the situation. In other words, self-compassion is remembering who you truly are and loving your true self, no matter what.

As you can tell, much has been written on this fascinating subject! But the more you understand self-compassion, the more you'll be motivated to bring yourself this miraculous gift. I've found that self-compassion is a practice built on these six core principles, which we'll return to again and again throughout this book:

1. SELF-AWARENESS. Self-compassion begins with knowing yourself. After all, how can we show ourselves compassion if we don't know the person we're being compassionate toward? Many of us walk through life without ever taking stock of who we truly are. But true self-awareness means perceiving oneself holistically—knowing your whole self, including the parts you don't like (we all have them). Exercises in this book will help you better understand your personal history and your current psyche, and become a neutral observer of your thoughts, feelings, and sensations during meditation. You'll learn a nonjudgmental approach to reflecting on how you came to be the person you are. When we are truly aware of ourselves, we have a greater ability to offer ourselves compassion. We come to live a life guided by the things we hold dear, not the things we fear.

2. **SELF-ACCEPTANCE.** In Buddhism, it's said that pain plus nonacceptance equals suffering. If you don't accept that a tree fell on top of your car, you'll never call the insurance company or a tow truck, you'll never get the tree removed or the car fixed, and you'll be stuck without transportation. Similarly, if we don't accept our flaws and shortcomings, we can't address and improve them. With self-acceptance, we fully embrace who we are, imperfections and all, without denial or shame. This doesn't mean we're complacent about our weaknesses; of course we should try to better ourselves. But it does mean that we don't let our failings get in the way of self-acceptance.

3. **EMPATHY AND UNDERSTANDING.** As a psychologist, I've seen firsthand how empathy and understanding can be powerful tools of healing and transformation. Think about how good it feels when you share your troubles with someone, and you can tell that they know exactly where you're coming from. The exercises in this book will help you get into the habit of applying this powerful force toward yourself. You'll learn to eliminate negative self-talk and find the positive in your experiences. For example, suppose you drop a glass. Instead of thinking "Why am I so clumsy?" self-compassion tells you "Accidents happen; I'm just glad I didn't hurt myself."

4. **KINDNESS.** This principle is at the heart of self-compassion. In fact, it's what usually comes to mind when people think of the concept. More than self-care, self-kindness includes a warm tenderness, incorporating a gentle approach to offering ourselves love through our thoughts and actions. And yet it's not always easy to apply, because for many of us, our thoughts tend to be more critical than kind. When you practice self-compassion, you learn to be gentle with yourself in the midst of pain—without ignoring or denying that pain.

5. PATIENCE. Self-compassion would not be complete without patience, which allows us to tolerate the inevitable difficulties and delays that plague us. Being patient with ourselves allows us the space to breathe, to feel less pressured by life, and to honor our unique journey. Patience gives us time to transform and to be our best selves in whatever divine timing the universe has in store for us. For example, perfectionist thinking might declare that you aren't achieving success fast enough—and cause you to stop trying. But fostering patience will allow you to achieve success in your own due time, with more joy along the way. With the patience of self-compassion, you accept that things take time, and that there's value in the journey.

6. PERSEVERANCE. Perseverance is the persistence in doing something despite difficulty or delay in achieving success. Sometimes called "grit," this aspect of self-compassion isn't always discussed—but it's important. We all need to persevere through tough times, and with self-compassion, we learn how to endure life's challenges without identifying with them. We come to understand that setbacks are not a confirmation of our inadequacy. Instead, we move forward through adversity and grow in the process. We learn to comfort ourselves through life's trials without giving up. We become resilient, better able to recover rapidly from difficulties.

What Self-Compassion Is Not

One of the reasons that self-compassion can be difficult to achieve is that the concept is often confused with other unrelated notions. Now that we know what self-compassion is, let's understand what it is not. Here are some common fallacies associated with self-compassion. Do any seem familiar? If you've come to this subject with your own biases and resistances, that's okay. Open yourself up to letting go of negative associations with self-compassion and honoring it for the gem that it is.

Self-compassion is not:

SELF-PITY. Some mistakenly confuse having compassion for yourself as an excuse to ruminate on one's troubles or burdens in an unhelpful way. On the contrary, self-compassion helps us overcome our troubles, as opposed to just wallowing in them. Kristen Neff explains that compassion trumps pity by offering a route to accepting life's challenges and the associated difficult feelings, versus feeling defeated by them.

SELF-INDULGENCE. Many people fear that offering themselves compassion may slide into overindulgence. However, self-compassion is not a free pass to indulge in instant gratification. It's a practice that requires thoughtful consideration of what's healthy and joyful for yourself—now and in the long run. When we offer ourselves compassion, we are taking time to offer ourselves truth and mindful consideration. That includes truths we may not want to hear but that are offered with kindness and love.

SELF-ESTEEM. Self-esteem is evaluation of our self-worth, typically determined by external factors such as accomplishments or popularity. But as we've touched on, self-compassion means honoring ourselves *in totality*, regardless of outside evaluations or material circumstances. Self-compassion is not conditional on what we've achieved in the world but is instead based on the important premise that we all deserve compassion. While self-compassion may lead to increased feelings of self-worth, it's in no way the same as externally based self-esteem. Self-compassion acknowledges our flaws and failings, while self-esteem disregards them.

LAZINESS. Self-compassion is not an excuse for neglecting one's responsibilities. In fact, it *enables* us to fulfill our obligations by helping us persevere and adding grace and flexibility to our efforts. Self-compassion encourages us to care for ourselves so we can function productively and maintain the motivation, energy, and confidence to honor our commitments and achieve our goals. And the practice of mindful self-compassion itself requires intention and effort.

SELFISHNESS. For some of us, the "self" in "self-compassion" brings connotations of selfishness, especially if we're highly self-critical. Sometimes "self" can be a loaded term! But it's important to remember that allowing ourselves compassion makes it possible to offer kindness to others. In fact, self-compassion thwarts narcissistic selfishness by increasing our capacity for kindness and empathy. You'll find as you engage with the exercises in this book that mindfully offering yourself compassion opens a new aptitude for you to offer compassion to others.

The Miracle of Mindfulness

No doubt you've come across the term "mindfulness" before. The concept has become mainstream, but it's an idea that's been taught for centuries by various religions, spiritual texts, and great philosophers. What was once thought of as an esoteric practice is now considered a valuable wellness tool that can bring anyone happiness. As we touched on earlier, mindfulness is a potent method for achieving self-compassion because it centers us on the present moment, where we can observe and understand ourselves. In fact, mindfulness is crucial for enacting the six principles of self-compassion discussed above.

What Is Mindfulness?

Many confuse mindfulness with meditation, but it's a broader concept than that. Think of it as a mental multi-tool that can be applied not only to meditating but also to activities of all sorts. Simply put, mindfulness is the act of focusing on the present moment and constantly bringing your attention back to the present moment when it has strayed. One might do that while meditating, but you could also do it while walking, driving, enjoying a meal—mindfulness can be practiced anytime, anywhere. It's a simple concept with profound implications. As with self-compassion, much has been written about the practice of mindfulness. A good way to deepen your understanding of the concept is to familiarize yourself with these seven core principles:

1. INTENTION. Mindfulness doesn't just happen. We *choose* to be mindful. It's a practice that requires a clear intention to initiate—the decision to take the time and energy to be mindful. By reading this book, you're already on the right track. You've set an intention to learn valuable skills so you can develop your own mindfulness practice. Your intention will be an asset as you maintain that practice and cultivate self-compassion.

2. PRESENT MOMENT AWARENESS. This is the defining quality of mindfulness: the ability to focus on the present moment and to continually bring your attention back when it wanders. Staying aware of the present moment can be incredibly healing. Anxiety usually pulls our attention to the future, while depression usually involves ruminating on the past. However, focusing on the present moment allows our worries and sorrow to dissipate or diminish.

3. REFLECTION. Once we bring our attention to the present moment, mindfulness encourages us to reflect on what we notice. This means taking note of our thoughts, emotions, body sensations, and behaviors, all as a way of deepening our acceptance and understanding of ourselves. Once you begin practicing mindfulness, you'll find yourself reflecting upon things you probably never noticed before, even in familiar surroundings or situations.

4. NONJUDGMENT. When we practice mindfulness, we must resist the urge to label what we notice as good or bad. Instead, we hope to encounter each moment with curiosity and reflect on it without judgment. As a tool for achieving self-compassion, mindfulness trains us to accept our whole self, rather than criticize the uncomfortable thoughts and emotions that are part of being human.

5. APPRECIATION. As we take in the present moment without judgment, the goal is for this mental stance to lead to an appreciation for each moment. Focusing on the present, we garner the ability to savor each instant for what it is. You'll find that the more you practice mindfulness, the more you'll appreciate the little things in life that used to pass by unnoticed. This type of gratitude cultivates increased happiness and joy every day. It also allows us to change our thinking patterns to focus more on the positive, even during difficult times.

6. OPENNESS. Mindfulness calls for us to open ourselves up to each sensation and thwart any inclinations to close ourselves off from any one experience. This willingness to experience what the present moment has to offer allows us to learn from life's difficulties and embrace life's pleasures. We're rewarded with a more complete experience in each moment.

7. COMPOSURE. Along with not judging the present moment, mindfulness teaches not to *attach* to what we experience. When a negative thought or difficult emotion arises, mindfulness keeps us calm and nonreactive. Maintaining composure allows us to be in control, able to experience our whole, authentic selves, and apply self-compassion whatever the challenges and tribulations of the day may be.

Mindfulness in Action: Mindfulness-Based Stress Reduction and Mindfulness-Based Cognitive Therapy

Don't let its ancient spiritual roots fool you; mindfulness has been scrutinized by modern science and embraced by contemporary medical practitioners. Psychology researchers have documented many benefits of practicing mindfulness, including decreased stress, anxiety, and sadness, as well as increased happiness and cognition (like better focus and memory). Moreover, the field of psychology has developed specific evidence-based therapy programs to bring these benefits to their patients.

One prominent example is called mindfulness-based stress reduction (MBSR), created by mindfulness pioneer Jon Kabat-Zinn, which teaches participants a variety of mindfulness techniques. Studies have found that MBSR significantly reduces stress and anxiety. Another treatment protocol, mindfulness-based cognitive therapy (MBCT), developed by psychology researchers Zindel Segal, Mark Williams, and John Teasdale, has been shown to significantly reduce depression. Other studies, such as that from Kathryn Birnie, Michael Speca, and Linda E. Carlson, have found that mindfulness programs are associated with decreased stress and mood disturbance and increased self-compassion, spirituality, and psychological functioning. There is substantial evidence that mindfulness and self-compassion go hand in hand and are quite effective in improving well-being.

Best Practices for Mindfulness Success

As a longtime practitioner of mindfulness, as well as a meditation teacher, I've developed a few strategies that have helped me stay consistent in, and gain the most benefits from, my own practice of mindfulness. To draw the most value from the mindfulness techniques you'll learn in this book, apply these strategies:

MAKE TIME. Even if you have a busy schedule—as so many of us do—I want to challenge you to change your notion of "I don't have time" to "I haven't made time." The truth is most of us have ample time to do the things that are important to us. The key is to *make* time. Prioritize your mindfulness practice to promote consistency and mastery.

MAKE A COMMITMENT. Reserving a block time for mindfulness each day will make your practice more habitual. For added success, try practicing at the same time of day. Also, for more formal mindfulness exercises like meditation, it may be helpful to designate a sacred space that is devoted to your practice. Any quiet place where you won't be disturbed or distracted will do.

KEEP A JOURNAL. I strongly encourage keeping a journal to enhance the benefits of your mindfulness practice. You'll find journal prompts throughout the book to help you go deeper with your self-reflection. Along with the prompts, as you practice the exercises in this book, take time after each to jot down any thoughts and emotions that arise. You can use whatever paper or digital format you're most comfortable with.

FORGET EXPECTATIONS. You may have come to this book with notions in your head of what mindfulness should look like. Forget them! Let go of any expectations and be open to your particular experience, however it unfolds. Allow yourself to have your own unique mindfulness journey, without comparing it to what you think is "supposed" to happen.

FIND A COMMUNITY. You don't have to do this alone. It can be very helpful to connect with others who practice mindfulness. You may find it helpful to enlist a friend to take this journey along with you. You might seek support or extra instruction with a mindfulness group, seminar, or class. Try searching online for meditation studios and mindfulness centers in your area.

Why Do It?
The Benefits of Mindfulness and Self-Compassion

How can a mindful self-compassion practice change your life? We can turn to a substantial body of research for answers. To further motivate your practice, here's a summary of some of the most promising benefits:

BETTER EMOTIONAL RESILIENCE. Life doesn't always have to be as hard as it seems. Sometimes it's all a matter of perception. Studies including that of Leary and others have shown that individuals with high levels of self-compassion are better able to handle life's difficulties, keep problems in perspective, and take responsibility for their contributing role to their problems. Mindful self-compassion improves our resilience, helping us face life's challenges and persevere through them, without becoming hardened.

REDUCED STRESS AND ANXIETY. We could all use less stress in our lives. Anxiety and stress contribute to poor health by over-activating our fight-or-flight system. When this happens, our bodies feel like they're under constant threat, which leads to an excess release of the stress hormone cortisol. And that wreaks havoc on our well-being. Not only has self-compassion been shown to deactivate our physiological reaction to stress, it activates the calming, soothing neural circuits in our brain. The result is a lower heart rate, improved digestion, and all sorts of health benefits that come when our bodies shift into relaxation mode.

REDUCED DEPRESSION. Self-compassion has been shown to reduce key symptoms of depression, such as rumination, isolation, and self-criticism. Self-compassion won't stop us from ever experiencing sadness, but it does seem to serve as a protective factor that keeps our sadness from festering into depression. It allows us to process our sad feelings and connect with them without letting them overcome us.

INCREASED HAPPINESS AND EMOTIONAL WELL-BEING. This may be the benefit that entices the most people to practice self-compassion: We all desire to feel happiness. Strong evidence shows that people with increased levels of self-compassion, as opposed to self-criticism, experience more happiness and feelings of love, joy, inspiration, and excitement more frequently.

IMPROVED SELF-WORTH. Because self-compassion stresses the importance of unconditional self-love and acceptance, it helps increase feelings of self-worth. Through self-compassion, we value ourselves for our intrinsic right to self-kindness and understanding.

THE END OF SELF-CRITICISM. Self-compassion is a powerful tool for defeating self-criticism. It replaces self-judgment with self-kindness, isolation with common humanity, and over-identification with observing. Negative self-talk such as criticism, judgment, and perfectionism only hinder our ability to be our best selves. Self-compassion eliminates this type of thinking and swaps in more helpful and empowering thoughts.

THE ABILITY TO DEAL WITH DIFFICULT EMOTIONS. Research shows that folks practicing self-compassion are less likely to avoid their emotions and are better able to cope with difficult emotions using strategies of acceptance and reflection. The ability to fully connect with our feelings—to acknowledge and accept them—allows us to use those emotions to grow, heal, and transform. Emotions are signals (we'll talk more about this in chapter 3), and self-compassion enables us to understand those signals instead of avoiding them.

IMPROVED MOTIVATION. Whatever your goals in life, self-compassion will be a great motivator, as it's correlated with improved self-efficacy, personal initiative, and intrinsic (that is, self-generated) motivation. Practicing self-compassion has been linked to one's motivation to change, try harder, and do better. It takes away the fear of making a mistake and allows us to try our best and learn from any mistakes we may make along the way.

How to Use This Book

Mindful Self-Compassion is intended to provide you with a holistic, whole-person approach to improving your well-being, one that serves body, mind, and spirit. To that end, each chapter is oriented toward supporting a specific aspect of the self. We will approach the mind by working on our thoughts (chapter 2), the spirit by working on our emotions (chapter 3), and the body by working on our self-care and body image (chapter 4). The final chapter will help you develop a plan to utilize self-compassion over the long term, adding daily practices to different aspects of your life. I've curated the exercises in this book not only to help you manage difficult thoughts, emotions, and body issues but also to foster positive experiences, enabling kinder thoughts, positive emotions, and body positivity.

You'll find that the 56 exercises in the following chapters are presented in a user-friendly, straight-to-the-point format. Each begins with notes on what the exercise is best used for and how much time to spend on it, followed by a brief description and step-by-step instructions. At the end of each chapter, there are also two journal prompts to promote mindful reflection that will help you gain the most value from your new mindfulness practice. The journal prompts are intended to inspire you to think more deeply about your practice of mindful self-compassion and to consider the best ways to use the insights you gain. You should also use your journal to record any thoughts or feelings that arise during the exercises. Some of the exercises also include a writing component. You can complete those in your journal, too, or record them elsewhere.

In each chapter, the first few exercises are particularly important, as they'll teach you to develop skills and understand concepts needed for more challenging exercises. After that, you can learn the other exercises in sequence, or prioritize the ones that seem most relevant to your situation. Unless you're very experienced with mindfulness practices, I suggest beginning your journey with the thought-based exercises in chapter 2. Our thoughts impact our emotions and our actions, so building a foundation of self-compassionate thoughts will help make the exercises in the later chapters much easier.

As your practice of mindful self-compassion progresses, you can use this list to return to the exercises that you've found to be particularly effective for specific circumstances.

◇ ANGER: Accepting All of You, chapter 2, page 46; Cooling the Flame, chapter 3, page 68; TIPPing point, chapter 4, page 112

◇ ANXIETY/STRESS: Use Your Superpowers, chapter 3, page 74; Creative Juices, chapter 5, page 144; A Handful of Bliss, chapter 4, page 94; Step by Step, chapter 4, page 116; Just Relax, chapter 4, page 96; Peace in a Box, chapter 3, page 78; Your True Self, chapter 2, page 42

◇ BURNOUT: Me First, chapter 3, page 82; Break Time, chapter 5, page 148

◇ CALMING DOWN/RELAXING: TIPPing Point, chapter 4, page 112; Just Relax, chapter 4, page 96; Bath Time Oasis, chapter 4, page 98

◇ CULTIVATING JOY AND PLEASURE: Laugh Out Loud, chapter 4, page 104; Taking in Your Good, chapter 2, page 44; Fun Time, chapter 5, page 140; Family First, chapter 5, page 132

We are what we think. All that
we are arises with our thoughts.
With our thoughts we make the
world.

—THE BUDDHA

Chapter 2

||||||||||||||||||||||||||||||||||||||||||||||||||||||||||||||||||||||||||||||||||

JUST A THOUGHT

Introduction

What is the origin of our inner critic—that voice that is forever telling us what we're doing wrong? You may find it surprising to hear that to keep us safe, our brains have evolved to pay more attention to negative thoughts such as judgments and self-criticism. Psychologist Rick Hanson describes this as "negativity bias." That is, our brains are wired to glom on to negative thoughts and repel positive ones. After all, when our ancestors were being chased by a saber-toothed tiger or trying to remember which berries were poisonous to eat, even a small mistake could have been deadly. However, in our modern, more complex world, this inclination toward negative thinking no longer serves us very well. Instead it perpetuates unproductive negative emotions such as sadness, fear, anger, and shame.

It's been said that we have between 12,000 and 50,000 thoughts a day. It's easy enough to let those thoughts run rampant without any consideration for how they affect us. But consider what pioneering psychiatrist Carl Jung once said: "Until you make the unconscious conscious, it will direct your life, and you will call it fate." Our thoughts affect our emotions and behaviors, and if we don't understand them, we risk allowing them to contribute to increased anxiety, depression, stress, and low self-esteem.

When it comes to negative thinking, one of the most important concepts you should understand is that you are not your thoughts. You are the person having your thoughts, but they do not define who you are. A goal of mindfulness is to detach from your thoughts, observe them neutrally, and not treat them as facts. This chapter will teach you to do that, so you can take stock of your thoughts and evaluate their impact on your mental well-being. Once you create some space between you and your thoughts, you may be amazed to see how much they affect your mood and daily life.

Our thoughts are fueled by our unconscious beliefs. With that in mind, this chapter also includes exercises to help you explore the unconscious notions that inhibit your capacity to be kind to yourself. You'll learn how to recognize negative beliefs and replace them with more helpful, healthy attitudes. Mindful self-compassion is a powerful force that can rewire our brains to experience joy, confidence, pride, love, and many other positive emotions. Using mindfulness, we have the power to counteract our inborn negativity bias and invite happiness and improved well-being into our lives.

Thought Bubbles

TIME: 5–10 minutes
BEST FOR: Decreasing self-judgment, increasing self-awareness

This mindfulness exercise will help you decrease self-judgment by teaching you to become an observer of your own thoughts, creating space between your thoughts and who you truly are. The goal is to become aware of your thoughts as they occur and take note of any themes that arise. When we observe our thoughts instead of attaching to them, we can more easily see that we are not our thoughts. We glean important information that will give us the power to change negative core beliefs and think more positively.

Steps

1. Take a comfortable seated position on a cushion or in a chair. Relax your arms and place your hands in your lap or on your knees.

2. Set a timer for 5 to 10 minutes. If you're new to mindfulness, I suggest beginning with a 5-minute duration and working your way up to 10 minutes by adding a minute each time you practice.

3. Close your eyes and take three deep breaths, inhaling through your nose and exhaling through your mouth.

4. Release control of your breath and allow your breathing to come to a slow, natural pace.

5. Without controlling your breath, simply notice the next three breaths you take. Pay attention to the physical sensations of your breathing.

6. Next, focus your attention on your thoughts. What are you thinking?

7. As a thought arises in your head, picture it as words in a thought bubble, like you'd see in a cartoon. A key aspect of this exercise is to not judge the thought as good or bad, but simply notice it from a neutral stance.

8. Then, without attaching to the sentiment of the thought, visualize the thought bubble drifting away, carrying the thought until it's no longer in your awareness.

9. Then wait for the next thought to arise.

10. Repeat the same process, seeing each thought as words in a bubble and letting it drift away.

11. In between arising thoughts, you may find it helpful to continue noticing your breath.

12. When your attention drifts to other sensations besides your thoughts or breath, just notice the sensation and gently bring your attention back to your thoughts or breath.

13. Continue this practice until the timer sounds.

Take the Leap

TIME: 10 minutes
BEST FOR: Increasing self-confidence, coping with guilt and shame

This exercise will help you address cognitive biases: thinking errors that affect your judgment and limit your ability to go after something you want. Cognitive bias happens when you let past circumstances or events override the evidence of the present moment. For example, you may decide not to attempt a new business venture because of a past failure, ignoring evidence that your new project could be very successful. This technique will help you take off the blinders of the past and release any guilt or shame for past mistakes. It will empower you to take a leap and go after something you want by strengthening your self-acceptance, empathy, patience, and perseverance.

Steps

1. Start by finding a quiet and comfortable space for reflection on a specific goal. You may find it useful to record your insights in your journal.

2. Next, set an intention to be open to a new experience. Write down a mantra, a statement of encouragement that you can repeat to stay motivated. For example, you might write "I am willing to invite new experiences into my life" or "I am determined to go after what I want."

3. Next, take a moment to consider how the evidence of the present situation relates to your goal. Make a list of any fears that are keeping you from pursuing what you want, and evaluate which fears are related to the past and which are connected to present circumstances. What is different about the current situation? How are you better prepared? What's working in your favor in the present moment? For example, if you want to go after a job promotion, you might worry that you won't be taken seriously. But you may have much more experience, and a track record of success, compared to the last time you sought a promotion.

4. Take a moment to reflect on how you can learn from past mistakes. If you went after a similar goal in the past but it didn't work out, what lessons did you learn? How can you apply those lessons to your current situation?

5. Now consider the worst that could happen as you pursue your goal. List everything that could go wrong and try to come up with a way to handle each. For instance, in pursuing a job promotion, you might find that the position's already been filled, that you don't have the qualifications, or that there are others being considered for the position. You might deal with these by keeping in contact with the hiring manager, rewriting your résumé to emphasize your skills and experience, or asking your boss if you can take on a project to show your ability.

6. End the exercise by taking time to reflect on the fact that challenges are opportunities to learn, not reflections of your ability. Develop a mantra that speaks to the fact that your worth is not dependent on your success—for example, "I am worthy of happiness regardless of my achievements or failures."

3 Bended Truth

TIME: 3 minutes
BEST FOR: Negative self-talk, negative thoughts, unhelpful thoughts

This is a quick mental strategy that you can do in your head to deal with negative self-talk and thoughts. These are often based on cognitive distortions, inaccurate thinking patterns that bend the truth to trap us in negativity. Here you'll learn some common cognitive distortions and a simple technique to escape the trap.

Steps

1. Prepare for this exercise by becoming mindful of your negative thoughts. Often, we don't even notice our negative self-talk because it's so habitual. Try using a notepad or recording app to capture negative thoughts when they occur.

2. When you're ready to examine your negative thoughts, sit in a quiet, comfortable place and examine the record you've kept.

3. Consult this list of common cognitive distortions, and consider which category each thought falls under:

   ✦ All or nothing thinking: "Either I do this perfectly, or not at all."

   ✦ Overgeneralizing: "Nothing ever works out for me."

   ✦ Disqualifying the positive (after receiving a compliment): "Anybody could have done that."

   ✦ Jumping to conclusions: "He must think I'm an idiot."

- Magnification: "If I don't get this job, my life is over."

- Emotional reasoning: "I feel ashamed, so I must be an awful person."

- Shoulds: "I should have done better"; "This should have worked out for me."

- Labeling: "I'm a failure."

- Personalization: "This is all my fault."

4. Add the words "I sometimes think" in front of each cognitive distortion: "I sometimes think I am a failure," or "I sometimes think this is all my fault." This will help create space between yourself and the thought, and remind you that it's just a thought, not a fact.

5. Next, add a contradicting statement to each, starting with the word "but." This statement should offer refuting evidence to balance your negative thought. For example, you might add "BUT there have been times in my past when I did succeed at things," or "BUT there are factors involved that I couldn't control."

6. Finally, add a self-compassionate statement that starts with the word "and." This statement should offer kindness while acknowledging your human right to love and understanding, for example, "AND my worth is not dependent on my success."

7. Now, repeat the entire final statement in your head or say it out loud: "Sometimes I think I am a failure, but there have been times in my past when I did succeed at things. And my worth is not dependent on my success." Return to the statement every time you find that negative thought arising.

STOP Uninvited Thoughts

TIME: 2 minutes

BEST FOR: Intrusive thoughts, triggering thoughts

Intrusive thoughts are like uninvited guests who, no matter what you do, just refuse to leave the party. These are unwanted thoughts, usually based in anxiety, that come into our mind and trigger fear, unease, and stress. But with mindful self-compassion, you can enjoy the party even with uninvited guests present. The STOP technique has many variations, but here's a mindfulness-based version that I developed to increase self-acceptance while also lessening the effect of triggering, intrusive thoughts. Use it to strengthen your ability to tolerate intrusive thoughts, increasing your capacity for self-compassion in the process. With kindness, patience, and self-awareness, this strategy will help you feel in control.

Steps

S: STOP AND OBSERVE THE THOUGHTS YOU ARE HAVING. Take three deep breaths as you become more aware of the thoughts as being separate from yourself. Mindfully focus your attention on the present moment and the arising thought.

T: TURN AWAY JUDGMENT. Resist any urges to judge yourself for the thoughts you're having. Accept thoughts for what they are and try not to devalue yourself for having them. Offer kindness to yourself as you observe your thoughts without drawing any conclusions.

O: OBSERVE YOUR REACTION TO THE THOUGHT IN THE MOMENT. What emotions do you feel? What body sensations are you experiencing? Notice what triggered you to have the intrusive thought—was it something you saw, something someone said? In this step, pause and take a moment to reflect on the context of this thought and how you responded to it.

P: PERSPECTIVE. Now step back and look at the bigger picture. Ask yourself, "Does this thought serve my higher purpose?" If not, gently focus on other thoughts that align with your values. Please note that the intrusive thought may still be present and that trying to force it to go away only gives it more power. In this step, simply bring in other positive thoughts that you can focus on instead. In doing so, the intrusive thought may fade, but that is not the goal. You're simply turning away from this unwanted guest to spend time with a more positive crowd. This negative thought does not define who you are.

Offer Yourself Love

TIME: 10 minutes

BEST FOR: Cultivating self-love and self-esteem

This loving-kindness meditation will help you experience exactly that. It's specifically designed to increase your self-compassion and feelings of warmth. The exercise is effective because it evokes your innate capacity to offer compassion to others, then redirects that ability toward yourself.

Steps

1. This meditation can be done either seated comfortably or lying down. Once comfortable, place one hand on your heart, and let the other hand rest gently on your belly.

2. Close your eyes and notice your breathing. Without controlling your breath, observe each inhalation and exhalation for 10 breaths.

3. As you follow the steps below, notice any emotions or body sensations that arise.

4. Picture the whole Earth floating in front of you. Visualize the world as a small sphere or globe.

5. With all the planet's beings, humans, animals, and plants in mind, offer the world love by speaking the following statements (out loud or in your mind; it's okay to read the statements off the page until you've memorized them):

   + May you experience joy and be free of suffering.

   + May you feel safe and beautifully flourish.

+ May you have good health and well-being.

+ May you prosper abundantly.

6. Reconnect with your breath. Without controlling your breathing, observe each inhalation and exhalation for 10 breaths.

7. Now recall someone you love. This can be a romantic partner, family member, a friend, or even a pet.

8. With your loved one in mind, offer love as you repeat the following:

+ May you experience joy and be free of suffering.

+ May you feel safe and beautifully flourish.

+ May you have good health and well-being.

+ May you prosper abundantly.

9. Again, reconnect with your breathing, observing 10 breaths without controlling them.

10. Now bring your attention to yourself. Keeping in mind what it felt like to offer others love, take a moment to offer yourself this same kindness and recite the following statements:

+ May I experience joy and be free of suffering.

+ May I feel safe and beautifully flourish.

+ May I have good health and well-being.

+ May I prosper abundantly.

11. Notice how it felt to offer yourself love and take note of any positive emotions that you experienced.

12. Close this meditation by taking three deep breaths.

Roster of Kindness

TIME: 5 minutes

BEST FOR: Negative self-talk, self-criticism, negative thoughts

This exercise will help you create long-lasting mind-set changes when practiced regularly. Thought records are commonly used in the psychology world to help individuals develop more positive thinking. In this case, the strategy is specifically intended to help you develop self-compassionate thoughts. You'll use the power of writing to ingrain new thinking pathways into your mind. The habit of mindfully observing your thoughts and balancing out negative core beliefs will lead to lasting positive shifts in the way you think.

Steps

1. Designate a notepad or digital device to carry with you and record your negative self-talk and self-criticism.

2. As you go about your day and notice negative self-talk, make it a habit to jot down the exact thought. Try to complete this exercise in the moment or as soon afterward as you can.

3. Underneath the thought, make five lines, numbered one through five.

4. On line one, jot down the situation in which the thought occurred. Where were you, what were you doing, what was happening around you? Take special note of anything that triggered this thought.

5. Then, on line two, write any underlying beliefs that seem related to the thought. For example, if the thought was "I'm lazy," the underlying belief might be "I don't deserve to relax." Use the journal prompt on page 50 to improve your ability to glean underlying beliefs.

6. On line three, write the emotions you felt after having this thought. Rate the intensity of the emotion on a scale from one (barely noticeable) to five (overwhelming).

7. On line four, write a compassionate statement in response to this thought. To make this statement most effective, address your negative core belief. Here are some tips to come up with your statement of compassion:

    ✦ What would a kind friend say to you if they heard you state that negative thought?

    ✦ Is there a more compassionate way to respond to the situation that triggered the thought?

    ✦ How can you offer yourself soothing kindness after having this thought?

8. On line five, describe how you feel after reading the compassionate statement. If the statement was particularly helpful, save it for future use.

Good Enough Mom

TIME: 2 minutes
BEST FOR: Coping after making a mistake, coping with guilt or shame, negative self-talk

We all make mistakes, and mistakes can be painful. But when we respond to our mistakes with negative self-talk and criticism, our pain is turned to suffering. This exercise uses self-compassion to help us process feelings of guilt and shame that can arise when we fail and puts them to use as tools for transformation. The term "good enough mother" was coined by psychoanalyst D. W. Winnicott. It describes a caring mother figure who is not perfect but balances meeting her child's needs with allowing enough frustration to help the child grow. We can develop our own internalized "good enough mother" voice within our psyche to help us through difficult times and emotions and guide us to more compassionate thoughts. Use this exercise to create your own inner "good enough mother," who will offer you compassion in the face of guilt and shame. Note the short time limit on this exercise; keep moving through the steps and don't let yourself get stuck in feelings of regret or guilt.

Steps

1. Find a quiet space to practice this mindful reflection exercise. Take notes in your journal if you think it may be helpful.

2. Start by acknowledging you have made a mistake. Be very honest with yourself about what that mistake is and how it does not align with your values.

3. Take accountability for the mistake. Whether it was a harmless error or it hurt someone else, reflect on your personal role in how this mistake happened.

4. Next, remind yourself that you are only human, and we all make mistakes. Offer yourself compassion by keeping in mind that we all deserve the opportunity to right our wrongs. Say to yourself, "One mistake does not define me."

5. Talk to yourself as a "good enough mother" would. Ask yourself how a loving mother might comfort you through your guilt. How would she hold you responsible for your mistake while also dissuading you from feeling ashamed? Practice talking to yourself in this way.

6. Next, draft a plan to make amends for your mistake. This may mean offering someone an apology or doing extra work to correct your error.

7. Finally, commit to avoid making this mistake again. Think about how to act in greater alignment with your values going forward. Do you need to be more diligent, plan more carefully, take others' feelings into consideration? Ask yourself what systems you can put in place to prevent future mistakes.

8 Overcoming Mountains

TIME: 5–10 minutes

BEST FOR: Facing daunting challenges, feeling defeated

Mindfulness can be incredibly effective for increasing grit, the strength to muster all your resolve and persevere through difficult situations. This self-compassion exercise focuses on improving your tenacity, building character, and strengthening resolve. Keep in mind that grit doesn't mean ignoring difficult feelings. A self-compassionate approach to grit can help you increase mental fortitude without beating yourself up in the process. Call on this guided visualization to cultivate compassionate strength.

Steps

1. Start by clearly identifying a specific obstacle you are trying to overcome. Define a related goal that aligns with your purpose. For example, if an obstacle is your anxiety over giving a presentation at work, your goal might be to conquer your fear of public speaking.

2. Take a moment to get into a comfortable seated position, close your eyes, and take three deep cleansing breaths.

3. Once you feel grounded, visualize yourself in the wilderness. Imagine that the obstacle you face is a huge mountain looming in front of you. (If a mountain is a difficult visualization for you, imagine a river you must swim across.)

4. Continue to take deep breaths as you envision yourself getting ready to climb this mountain. For motivation, think about how conquering this mountain will transform you in ways that will bring you closer to your life's goals.

5. Next, see yourself climbing the mountain. Visualize yourself on the mountainside and feel the effort in your arms and legs as you climb upward. Tap into feelings of pride as you make it closer and closer to the mountaintop. Compliment yourself for being brave enough to face this challenge.

6. After watching yourself climb for a few moments, imagine pausing your ascent to look back at how far you've come. And take another moment to recall moments in your personal life when you persevered and overcame a difficult challenge.

7. Refocusing on your visualization, further motivate yourself by envisioning what it will be like to reach the other side of this mountain. See yourself on the other side of this large obstacle and rejoice with confidence in your ability to do so. Then imagine yourself finding the internal strength and picture yourself working your way up the mountain, step by step, until you reach the top.

8. End this exercise by envisioning what it will be like to overcome your real-life challenge. Think about how you will feel. Consider how you've grown as a person in order to persevere through this challenge.

Strengths Spotlight

TIME: 10 minutes

BEST FOR: Low self-confidence, defeating self-criticism

Many of us spend plenty of energy trying to become better people and working to improve our weaknesses— and that's a good thing. But unfortunately, expending so much effort on our faults can overshadow our positive attributes. In fact, rarely do people ever take time to consider their strengths. This is a simple exercise to help you stay mindful of your strengths by creating a positive inventory you can refer to when your confidence is low. This process acknowledges that while our worth is not based on self-evaluations, there's value in taking an opportunity to honor the best in us. If feelings of discomfort or guilt arise along the way, do your best to just notice these feelings without attaching to them, and push through to complete the exercise.

Steps

1. Gather a pen and paper or your journal, and find a comfortable space for writing.

2. Title your page Strengths Spotlight.

3. Divide your page into three columns.

4. In the first column, list at least 15 personal strengths. List things you like about yourself and things you have noticed that you excel at. Include a variety by considering different domains of your life: work, family, hobbies, the emotional intelligence that you bring to friendships and relationships, and so on.

Think about your greatest accomplishments and recall any situations where you felt proud of yourself.

5. In the second column, write down at least 15 things that you think your friends and family appreciate about you. Suppose someone was introducing you to a stranger; what positive attributes about you might they share? What compliments do you commonly receive from others? If this column is difficult for you, I challenge you to call up a few loved ones and ask them what they think you're good at. This has been an eye-opening experience for many of my patients and can bring your attention to strengths you never knew you had.

6. Finally, in the last column list at least 15 reasons why you are amazing, regardless of your strengths or weaknesses. Call on your spiritual beliefs, if that applies, to validate your worthiness beyond self-evaluation. For instance, you might write down "Everyone deserves to feel good about themselves." Come up with at least 15 statements that validate your divine, innate worthiness.

7. End this exercise by taking time to review each column. Notice how it feels to put a spotlight on your strengths. Do you feel any resistance to allowing yourself to feel good? Try your best to be open to appreciating yourself. Return to this list whenever you're feeling self-critical and doubtful.

10 Your Own Best Friend

TIME: 10–15 minutes
BEST FOR: Low self-esteem, self-deprecating thoughts

Sometimes it's difficult to find the words to convey self-compassion. This exercise is a strategy to help you articulate kindness and empathy toward yourself at a difficult time when you're unsure how to start or what to say. It kickstarts the process by capitalizing on your ability to be compassionate with loved ones.

Steps

1. When you find you're being hard on yourself, take a moment to pause and ground yourself by connecting with your breath. Then notice your thoughts nonjudgmentally, and remind yourself that they are just thoughts, not facts.

2. Set yourself in a quiet and comfortable space where you can comfortably self-reflect and write without interruption. Gather a writing implement and paper (if you use an electronic device, create two separate pages to write on).

3. Use one page to write yourself a letter about the difficult situation you're currently in. Compose it from the perspective of your best friend. What might they say to comfort you in this circumstance? What might they say in response to your self-critical thoughts? Use the warm tone of a concerned best friend, and channel how that person might convey love and understanding for what you're going through. It can be helpful to picture the friend in your mind, and imagine hearing their voice, as you write this letter.

4. When you've completed the first letter, flip the page over (if you're working on paper). Now write a letter *to* your best friend. For this letter, imagine your friend is in the difficult situation that you're experiencing and voicing the self-critical statements you've been making. What might you say to comfort your friend? What evidence might you provide them to refute their critical thoughts? How would you try to make them feel better and cheer them up? What might you say to remind them of their strengths? It can be helpful to imagine yourself saying this directly to your friend; you can even speak your supportive words out loud.

5. Finish by taking time to carefully read both letters. Let the words sink in and allow yourself to feel the positive emotions that arise as you read these compassionate words. If you find this exercise particularly helpful, keep these letters close and reread them when you're feeling down about yourself.

11 Your True Self

TIME: 5 minutes

BEST FOR: Disconnecting from mind chatter

Connecting with your authentic self—your ultimate and pure identity, separate from thoughts and defenses—is a powerful way to cultivate self-compassion. Remember, we all have an intrinsic right to self-compassion, but sometimes we lose sight of that. When that happens, this exercise will help you reconnect to the calm and peaceful part of you that lies beyond your fleeting thoughts, emotions, and behaviors. By taking time to clarify and get in tune with your values, you can connect with what's truly important to you. Use this technique to align with the eternal part of you and honor your true self.

Steps

1. Find a quiet space and take a comfortable seated position. Close your eyes and focus on relaxing your body from head to toe. Take a few deep breaths and try to release any tension you notice.

2. Bring your awareness inward, and connect with your inner observer, noticing that you are observing your thoughts and emotions, and that your identity is separate from them. Try to disconnect from thoughts and sensations, and take a few breaths to simply notice them.

3. As you sit, connected to your inner observer, take a moment to reflect on your values. What's important to you in life? Is it peace, love, justice, creativity? Whatever they may be, take a moment to consider these values.

4. Now think about what motivates you in life. What gets you excited? What inspires you? Is it art, music, nature? Spending time with family, pursing a hobby, expressing yourself creatively?

5. Check in with your body and continue to release any tension you may notice.

6. Now recall the people in your life whom you admire. What attributes make you admire these people? What characteristics do you value about them?

7. Continue to relax your body. Observe any thoughts, emotions, or sensations that may have distracted you, and gently bring your attention back to reflecting on your values.

8. Consider what you aspired to be when you were a child, what you wanted to be when you grew up. What did you value about the life that you imagined for yourself?

9. Finally, consider your ideal self, the person you aspire to be now. Imagine this person and the life they lead. What strikes you most about this person and how they live? What makes this version of yourself ideal?

10. End the meditation by reflecting on all the values you have identified. Consider how these values ring true, no matter what the situation. Think about how you can move closer to these values in your daily life and, in the process, fully embody your authentic self.

12 Taking in Your Good

TIME: 1 minute

BEST FOR: Increasing feelings of joy and self-compassion, positive thinking

True self-compassion involves more than getting rid of the negative. It must include cultivating positive thoughts and experiences as well. Psychologist Rick Hanson teaches a mindfulness practice called "taking in the good" that helps individuals experience more joy and circumvents our brain's negativity bias (mentioned at the beginning of this chapter). This exercise builds on Hanson's method to help you increase moments of joyful self-compassion. You can use this mindfulness technique throughout your day, turning small moments into opportunities to increase your joy and self-appreciation. The more you practice it, the more you'll wire your brain to notice the good things and offer yourself compassion.

Steps

1. Set an intention to mindfully consider small moments of your own goodness throughout the day. Take note every time you take care of yourself or help others. This can be something as simple as eating a healthy lunch or holding the door for someone. In your mind, pat yourself on the back for little victories and niceties throughout the day.

2. When you notice something good about yourself, take a second to truly enjoy it. Relish in your own goodness and savor the feeling of self-appreciation. Pause and allow yourself to feel

good. Notice any resistance to feeling good about yourself and allow yourself to tap into self-appreciation anyway.

3. Next, let this good feeling sink in. For about 30 seconds, let this goodness run over you. Imagine a warm sense of joy running through your body from head to toe. Slow down your thoughts and enjoy these 30 seconds of bliss, and truly take in the moment of goodness as you visualize joy expanding within you.

4. Finally, notice how you feel after you focused your attention on your goodness. Do you feel different than before the exercise? Pausing to savor your own goodness throughout the day helps get your mind in the habit of self-appreciation. The more you practice this exercise with intention, the more your brain will naturally pause to take in the good.

13 Accepting All of You

TIME: 10 minutes

BEST FOR: Shame, anger, overcoming past mistakes

In previous exercises we focused on acknowledging your strengths, but self-compassion also means accepting your weaknesses. The Japanese aesthetic principle of wabi-sabi proclaims that accepting imperfection is a route to making the most out of life. This mindfulness technique follows that concept to help increase self-acceptance regardless of your flaws. It calls for you to confront what you may not like about yourself and honor yourself anyway. We all deserve compassion, and with this exercise you'll come to embrace your weaknesses as you offer yourself kindness.

Steps

1. This exercise is best done in a quiet space and in a comfortable seated position.

2. Begin by taking 10 deep breaths, inhaling through your nose and exhaling through your mouth. Then gently release control and breathe normally.

3. Recall a personal attribute of your own that you are working to improve. Once you have something in mind, say to yourself, "Even if I never change this about myself, I will love myself regardless, because we are all worthy of love. I accept all of me, flawed and all. There is beauty in imperfection."

4. Then, reflect on a past mistake that may have caused you some guilt. Once you have this in mind, say to yourself, "Every human makes mistakes, and nobody is perfect. I love myself regardless, because we are all worthy of love. I accept all of me, flawed and all. There is beauty in imperfection."

5. Think of something you wish you were better at, whether it be a learned skill or innate ability. Say to yourself, "I wouldn't be me without my own unique set of strengths and weaknesses. I love myself regardless, because we are all worthy of love. I accept all of me, flawed and all. There is beauty in imperfection."

6. Finally, think of a physical trait that you wish were different. Now say to yourself, "I am beautiful just the way I am. I love myself because we are all worthy of love. I accept all of me, flawed and all. There is beauty in imperfection."

14 It Takes Time

TIME: 10 minutes
BEST FOR: Impatience, curing the need for instant gratification

In today's world, with technology that speeds everything up and so many depictions of "overnight success," we're spoiled by how easily we can satisfy our craving for instant gratification. Doesn't it seem that patience is a virtue many of us lack? Cultivating self-compassion reveals that patience is actually a superpower; Buddhism considers patience to be an act of self-compassion that leads to peace and contentment. And the ability to tolerate delays helps us navigate a world that is not always on our schedule. The best way to increase your capacity for patience is surprisingly simple: practice waiting. Perform this exercise regularly to strengthen your ability to be patient, and call on it when you find impatience taking hold of your thoughts and emotions.

Steps

1. Throughout this exercise, pay special attention to any feelings of impatience or a desire to rush the process. Noticing these urges without giving in to them will further improve your ability to be patient.

2. Find a comfortable seated position either in a chair or on the floor. Relax your body and place your hands in your lap. (If you can't leave the setting you're in, perform the steps as best you can.)

3. Set a timer for 10 minutes.

4. Begin this exercise by closing your eyes and bringing your attention to your breath.

5. As you concentrate on your inhales and exhales, begin to count. Notice one inhalation and say, "One"; then, after you exhale, say, "One."

6. On the next breath, notice the inhalation and say, "Two," and following the exhalation, repeat, "Two."

7. Continue counting until you reach 10 breaths, and then start over.

8. Continue breathing and counting in this way until the timer sounds. Try not to rush your breathing, and try to resist any urges to finish the meditation early. Become the mindful observer of your breath, with patience to sit with each breath in the present moment.

9. If you notice that you go over 10 or lose count, resist any urge to judge yourself. Simply restart from one and continue trying. This is an exercise that requires concentration and takes practice to master. So be gentle with yourself along the way.

REFLECTION ONE

Revealing the core beliefs that underlie our negative thoughts is crucial for developing self-compassion. We have to uncover our negative core beliefs so we can develop more compassionate ones. In your journal, write down a negative thought you've had recently, and ask yourself, "What does this say about me?" Write down the answer, and then apply the same question to it. Repeat until you've drilled down to a negative core belief. For example, you might start with, "I'll never be able to land my dream job." What does this say about me? "Things don't work out for me." What does that answer say about me? "I don't have what it takes." Core belief: "I'm not good enough."

REFLECTION TWO

In the journal prompt on the previous page, you were encouraged to unmask negative core beliefs. Using the information you uncovered, write down positive beliefs that refute each of the negative ones. This will help you foster self-kindness in the face of negative thoughts and beliefs. Use these new positive core beliefs as mantras, repeating them to yourself when the negative beliefs arise.

When our emotional health is
in a bad state, so is our level of
self-esteem. We have to slow
down and deal with what is
troubling us, so we can enjoy
the simple joy of being happy
and at peace with ourselves.

—JESS C. SCOTT

Chapter 3

EMOTIONAL RESCUE

Introduction

Anger, sadness, fear—often we think of our negative emotions as
the enemy. We avoid them at all cost. But as unpleasant as they
feel, as difficult as they can be to experience, the reality is that these
emotions present themselves for our benefit, so that we can heal.
Positive or negative, emotions are not something we should dread,
or even try to control (though at times we need to exert control to
respond appropriately). Remember, from chapter 1, the Buddhist
wisdom that pain plus nonacceptance equals suffering? When we
avoid or ignore negative emotions, we suffer, and the effects can
impact our relationships, our productivity, our self-image, and our
overall quality of life. We need to accept these feelings instead,
listen to what they tell us, process them, and learn from them.

Emotional suffering can express itself in many ways: flying off
the handle; feeling too defeated to talk to anyone; developing perfectionist tendencies that generate guilt and shame; and battering
ourselves with negative self-talk. Sometimes we overindulge in an
emotion, leading to outbursts of anger or bouts of deep sadness.
Or we may use emotional eating or drinking to avoid a problem
at hand.

But ultimately, emotions are signals. Negative emotions and feelings are simply cues from our authentic self that something we're
thinking or doing is unwelcome and may not be in alignment with
our values. The emotional signals that demand our attention arise
from our perception of events, rather than the events themselves.
Someone who lost their job, for example, might view that loss as
an opportunity to try something new, and feel positive emotions
of relief, excitement, or anticipation. Someone else in the same

situation might focus on being treated unfairly and experience anger, frustration, or fear. In that case, mindful self-compassion allows us to examine those negative thoughts and search for a more positive way to react to that event.

We have limited control of the events of our lives, but self-compassion can help us manage how we respond to them. Mindful self-compassion creates a crucial pause between feeling your emotions and processing them, a space of clarity where you can assess those emotional signals more deeply before responding. In this chapter, you'll discover not only how to use mindful self-compassion to cope with negative emotions but also how to understand these signals and use them to your advantage. You'll discover meaning in your emotional experiences and learn to respond by realigning with what's important to you. You'll also develop the skill to access other, more positive emotions when you need them. Negative emotions will no longer dominate your experience. You'll become empowered to feel other emotions simultaneously: joy in the face of sorrow, calmness in the face of anger, and confidence in the face of fear.

Wave of Emotions

TIME: 10 minutes

BEST FOR: Feeling overwhelmed by emotion or feeling disconnected from emotional experience

Identifying your emotional state is an important first step in coping with difficult emotions, especially when you feel overwhelmed by them or disconnected from them. In this guided meditation, you'll use mindfulness and the basic principles of self-compassion to begin managing difficult emotions. This mindful self-compassion exercise will increase self-awareness and empower you to connect with your emotions in a safe way.

Steps

1. Find a quiet space where you can sit comfortably. You can do this meditation seated in a chair, with your hands palms up resting on the top of your thighs, or sitting on a pillow, blanket, or rug, cross-legged with hands resting palms up on your knees. Set a timer for 10 minutes.

2. Close your eyes and bring your attention to your breath. Notice each inhalation and exhalation. As you breathe, imagine an ocean tide that flows in as you inhale, and see the tide going out again as you exhale. Spend a minute using this ocean breathing technique, bringing in the ocean when you inhale and sending it out again when you exhale.

3. Shift your attention and notice what emotions are present in your mind. What feelings are washing over you? Once you notice an emotion, label it. Is it sadness, nervousness, anger,

joy? Notice where and how you feel this emotion in your body: Are your shoulders tense? Does your chest feel tight?

4. After fully connecting with the emotion, offer yourself compassion in the moment with the following mantra: "Right now I am feeling [insert emotion]. In my human experience, it is normal for me to have feelings. I offer myself love and know that this feeling will not last forever." Take a moment to notice how you feel after using the mantra.

5. Try not to dwell on the emotional experience. Turn your attention back to ocean breathing for another minute.

6. Shift your attention again to noticing the next rising emotion. It's okay if you are still feeling the same emotion.

7. Repeat the above mantra, followed by ocean breathing.

8. Repeat the cycle until your timer sounds.

Anthesis

TIME: 10 minutes

BEST FOR: Accepting difficult emotions

Accepting, rather than avoiding, our difficult emotions is a key part of emotional regulation. The steps in this exercise follow the six principles of acceptance and commitment therapy (ACT), created by psychologist and University of Nevada professor Steven Hayes, and help you accept difficult emotions without being overcome by them. Over time, this meditation will cultivate your willingness to experience difficult emotions using mindfulness and self-compassion. Its title, "anthesis," refers to the opening of a flower bud.

Steps

1. Find a quiet space to sit comfortably, in a chair or on a floor pillow.

2. **Connect** with the present moment. Close your eyes and start to observe your breath. For a minute, stay connected with each breath in the present moment, feeling the sensations without trying to control your breathing. If your mind wanders, gently bring your attention back to your breath.

3. **Accept.** Notice how you're feeling right now. Take a moment to identify the strongest emotion you feel, and give it a color that feels appropriate. Next, visualize a long-stemmed rose with a closed bud. Imagine that the rose is the color that you gave to your emotion. Picture your colored rosebud, and be willing to truly feel the emotion you are experiencing.

4. **Defuse.** Notice any thoughts that accompany this emotion. Then, use positive self-talk that separates you from your thoughts: "These are just thoughts, not facts." Now visualize your rosebud opening ever so slightly.

5. **Speak** to yourself. Tell yourself, out loud or in your mind, "I am not these emotions, I am not these thoughts. My true self is so much greater than this fleeting experience." Contemplate the truth that you are only the observer of these emotions and thoughts; they do not define you. Imagine your rosebud opening just a little bit more.

6. **View** your values. Shift your attention to what's most important to you in life. Reflect on some of your personal values: peace, happiness, family, honesty, spirituality, or whatever means the most. Visualize your rosebud opening even more, almost completely.

7. **Commit.** With your values in mind, think about how you can take steps to align with your values in the face of your difficult emotion. What actions can bring you closer to what's important to you, even when carrying emotional pain with you? Visualize your rose completely open and fully bloomed. This image symbolizes your openness to accept difficult emotions while still flourishing.

3 Let It RAIN

TIME: 5 minutes
BEST FOR: Allowing difficult emotions like sadness and anger

We can find many unhealthy ways to avoid our emotions: drinking, oversleeping, being overcontrolling, or even becoming a busy workaholic. Whatever the method, avoiding our emotions only makes our problems worse. Here's a mindfulness strategy that will help you connect with challenging feelings and gain greater awareness into why they've shown up. This mindfulness reflection technique is based on a strategy developed by meditation teacher Michele McDonald, cofounder of the Vipassana Hawai'i meditation retreat. I have adapted it to include tenets of self-compassion. Call on this mindful reflection anytime you're troubled by a negative emotion. It can be practiced wherever you are, with eyes open or closed. Use the acronym RAIN to remember this technique.

Steps

R: RECOGNIZE. Start by taking a moment to recognize what emotion you're feeling in this moment. Try to put a name to your emotion. For example, after missing a deadline you might say, "I am frustrated." Notice any body sensations that accompany it. It can be helpful to repeat the emotion in your mind once you notice it: "Frustration, frustration, frustration." This helps to wrap your brain around what you are really feeling.

A: ALLOW. Consciously work to give yourself permission to feel the emotion. Notice any resistance, and gently encourage yourself to allow the emotional experience. To create an accepting space for this emotional experience, try saying, "I allow myself to feel this emotion and know that it will help me in the long run. I am open. I am willing. I will survive this experience."

I: INVESTIGATE. Gently investigate what triggered this emotion. Think about the contributing situation, behaviors, and thoughts that accompany it. Offer yourself compassion as you investigate, keeping in mind that the more you learn about the trigger of this feeling, the more power you have to process this emotion and move on. During this phase, you may also notice other emotions. For example, your investigation may uncover sadness underneath your anger, or fear underneath your embarrassment.

N: NON-IDENTIFY. Finally, remind yourself that your identity is not what you are feeling. Increase your self-awareness by keeping in mind that you are the person feeling the emotion, not the emotion itself.

Cushioning the Blow

TIME: 5–10 minutes
BEST FOR: Softening difficult emotions

Difficult emotions challenge us every day. Negative feelings can arise as we're forced to deal with the unavoidable stressors of life, from missing your train to a high-pressure work deadline. Learning how to tolerate feelings such as frustration or anxiety, particularly when they're evoked by situations you can't change, is a key to emotional regulation. Dialectal behavioral therapy (DBT), a therapy created by psychologist Marsha Linehan to build and improve emotional regulation, lends us many tools to help tolerate difficult emotions in the moment. This version of the DBT IMPROVE skill uses mindful self-compassion to help you tolerate the distress caused by difficult emotions as you move through the pain.

Steps

When you're experiencing a difficult emotion, find a quiet space to complete this exercise. If needed, practice it wherever you are, as long as you can safely concentrate. The IMPROVE acronym will help you remember the steps.

I: IMAGERY. Start by identifying the situation—"I'm angry at my friend," for example, or "I feel like giving up"—and the trigger that has caused this emotion. Don't spend a lot of time analyzing; just go with what first comes to mind. Was it someone's critical comment, a bad memory, an unexpected delay? Then imagine yourself coping successfully with this situation. What would you say and do?

M: MEANING. Next, try to make meaning out of the situation you're in, using self-compassion. Start by offering yourself empathy and understanding; accept that it's okay you had this emotional reaction. Then try to find meaning in what this moment has to teach you. Have you learned to stick up for yourself when criticized or to give yourself more time to complete a task?

P: PRAYER. Ask for strength to see you through as you process this difficult emotion. Your appeal could be a prayer in the religious sense or simply a plea to an unknown higher power, the universe, your best self, or whatever fits your values.

R: RELAXATION. Offer yourself compassion in the form of self-care. Take a moment to engage in a simple relaxation technique to help calm your nerves. Opt for something that's easy and convenient to the situation, such as taking 10 deep breaths, drinking hot tea, giving yourself a hand massage (see chapter 4, page 94), or listening to calming music.

O: ONE THING IN THE MOMENT. Take a moment to mindfully do one thing, and one thing only, mentally zeroing in on what you're doing in your moment of emotional distress. If you're driving, for example, pay complete attention to that. Focusing on a single activity will help further calm you.

V: VACATION. Take a self-compassionate mental vacation in your mind. Imagine yourself somewhere joyful and safe. Put yourself there for a minute or two, whether it's a walk on the beach or an evening at home, snug in your bed.

E: ENCOURAGEMENT. End the exercise with positive self-talk that will encourage you to push through this difficult time. Try saying something like "I can get through this" or "I have what it takes to tolerate this pain and come out better on the other side."

5 One-Two-Three Break

TIME: 6 minutes

BEST FOR: Feeling down after negative self-talk, dealing with emotions resulting from your inner critic

The judgmental thoughts of the inner critic can trigger negative emotions such as shame and sorrow. Sometimes these emotions are overwhelming. This exercise offers a mindful way to cope with the emotional aftermath of the inner critic, counteracting its effects with the power of self-compassion.

Steps

1. When you notice mind chatter dominated by negative self-talk, stop what you're doing and take six minutes for a self-compassion break.

2. Find a quiet space to reflect. This exercise is best performed sitting down, either in a chair or on the floor.

3. Take one minute to engage in this breathing technique for stress reduction:

   + Inhale deeply through your nose, as if you're smelling a rose.

   + Breathe deeply into your belly so that your diaphragm expands. This reduces distress by sending a signal to your brain that you are safe.

- Hold the breath for a second or two.

- Exhale fully through your mouth, as if you were blowing out a birthday candle.

4. Take two minutes to make these statements, out loud or in your mind. Repeat the breathing technique after each statement:

- I accept myself.

- I know I am not this emotion.

- Feeling this way is difficult.

- I offer myself love in this moment.

- This feeling won't last forever.

- I know I will persevere.

5. Take three minutes to reflect on the following to cultivate positive feelings:

- For one minute, think about all the things that bring you joy.

- For one minute, think about all the things that make you laugh.

- For one minute, think about all the people that care about you now and have cared about you in the past.

6. Use this technique as many times as you need to throughout the day. Be sure to notice how you feel before and after.

Daily Compassion Check-In

TIME: 10 minutes

BEST FOR: Training your brain to be more compassionate

An amazing aspect of self-compassion is that it builds on itself. By becoming more conscious of how often we engage in compassionate thinking, we become more likely to improve this healthy habit. This exercise is designed to increase your self-awareness and to instill in your brain how it feels to be compassionate. By tracking self-compassion daily, you'll take note of the benefits you experience and become more likely to engage in this type of thinking in the future. The result: more frequent feelings of happiness, love, and peace.

Steps

1. Create a plan to make this compassion check-in a part of your daily routine. I suggest adding it to your bedtime ritual by keeping a notepad by your bedside. You can use your self-compassion journal or keep a separate record.

2. Take about 10 minutes to answer the following questions about your day, elaborating on your answers with as much detail as you can.

    ✦ Was I able to notice my inner critic or negative self-talk in the moment? Here are some examples of negative and critical self-talk:

        ◇ Judging yourself for your flaws or weaknesses

        ◇ Being intolerant of your emotional experience

- ◇ Being impatient with yourself

- ◇ Imposing perfectionist thinking on yourself

- ◇ Calling yourself names

- ◇ Imposing unrealistic expectations on yourself

✦ Was I able to offer myself compassion when I noticed self-critical thinking?

✦ How did it feel when I noticed negative self-talk? How did it feel to offer myself compassion?

✦ When I felt difficult emotions, was I able to accept them and allow them into my experience?

✦ When I encountered difficult situations, was I able to add meaning and understanding to my experience?

✦ Was I able to be patient with myself as I experienced difficult emotions or challenges?

✦ Was I able to offer myself encouragement to persevere through the day's challenges?

✦ Did I find ways to compliment myself throughout the day?

✦ Was I able to be kind and warm toward myself throughout the day?

✦ Did I do things to take care of myself today?

✦ Was I able to notice myself feeling positive after being compassionate toward myself?

✦ Overall, did I engage in self-compassionate thinking and behaviors throughout the day?

Cooling the Flame

TIME: 10 minutes
BEST FOR: Experiencing anger

Self-compassion is an excellent way to cope when anger flares up. It can calm us down and also help us discover the underlying feelings that fueled the fire. This mindfulness reflection strategy encourages compassion in the face of irritability, anger, or rage, helping you pause and reconnect with your true self. It builds self-compassion by increasing self-awareness, self-kindness, and empathy.

Steps

1. Start by noticing the emotions you are feeling. Rate your anger on a scale of 1 to 10. Then notice how anger has manifested in your body. Are your fists clenched? Are you sweating? Has your heart rate increased? Have you clenched your jaw or are you grinding your teeth? Do you feel dizzy? Are you trembling?

2. Use slow, controlled breathing to soothe yourself. Inhale through your nose to the count of 10, taking a deep belly breath that expands your diaphragm. Then hold your breath for a count of 5. Finally, release the breath, exhaling through your mouth for a count of 10.

3. Continue breathing this way for two full minutes.

4. Next, release control of your breath and close your eyes. Reflect on the source of your anger. What situation triggered this emotional reaction?

5. Name what sparked your irritation, and say to yourself, "I have the right to feel angry." Notice any other feelings that accompany the anger. Ask yourself if it's easier to feel this anger than the underlying sadness, disappointment, fear, or other feelings. Can you open yourself to fully experiencing all the emotions you notice, not just your anger?

6. Repeat your slow, controlled breathing. Inhale to the count of 10, hold for 5, then exhale for 10. Breathe in this way for another two minutes.

7. Shift your attention to how you can act with positive intent in the face of this anger. Ask yourself how, in this moment, you can align with your purpose in life. Can you take steps to address the problem that triggered your anger? If it can't be avoided, can you prepare for the situation so it won't be problematic next time?

8. End the reflection with a final round of slow, controlled breathing for two minutes.

Only Human

TIME: 5 minutes
BEST FOR: Coping with embarrassment or shame after a mistake

When your inner critic encourages you to beat yourself up over a mistake, feelings of guilt, embarrassment, and shame can follow. This exercise helps you cope with these difficult emotions, replacing them with self-acceptance, patience, and understanding. You'll learn self-compassion mantras that will empower you to appreciate your authentic self.

Steps

1. Start by labeling any feelings of guilt, embarrassment, or shame that you're experiencing. Notice if you're being hard on yourself with negative self-talk. Observe the domain of your life (e.g., work, home, leisure activities, personal relationships) in which this mistake took place. Try to paint a clear picture of what you are feeling and how that feeling manifested.

2. Next, recite the following mantras, in your mind or out loud, to create space for self-compassion, grace, and forgiveness. Take time to truly feel the meaning of the words and let their significance sink in. After each statement, take three deep breaths, and move on to the next mantra.

   + Kindness mantra: May I be kind to myself. May I be happy. May I let myself off the hook. May I hold this situation lightly. May I be open to letting this feeling run its course without clinging to it.

+ Empathy mantra: I understand how I came to feel this way. It is okay to experience negative emotions. It's not easy facing such tough emotions. It's understandable to feel pain.

+ Humanity mantra: I am only human. All humans make mistakes. Pain is a part of the human experience. It's normal to have weaknesses.

+ Authentic-self mantra: I am a divine soul having a human experience. Mistakes are part of that experience, and my worth is not dependent on never making them. The sum of my life, including both successes and mistakes, creates the magnificence of my true being.

+ Gratitude mantra: I am grateful for this experience. I know this experience can teach me and help me grow as a person. I appreciate the ability to feel gratitude in the face of difficult emotions.

9 Your Big Win

TIME: 10 minutes

BEST FOR: Handling feelings of defeat or disappointment

There are situations in life that can leave us feeling crushed. Hopelessness can soon creep in, making it hard to know what to do next. This mindfulness exercise helps you boost self-compassion in times of defeat. It teaches you how to process your disappointment and bring feelings of hope into your experience. Through this visualization, you will cultivate patience, resilience, and self-kindness, which will help you overcome a setback and focus on your future big win.

Steps

1. Find a calm space and take a comfortable position, either seated or lying down.

2. Close your eyes.

3. Try to relax your entire body. Pay special attention to relaxing your eyes, jaw, shoulders, and belly.

4. Place your hand on your belly and take 10 deep belly breaths, feeling your hand rise and fall each time as your belly expands and contracts.

5. Gently return to normal breathing, and take a moment to notice if you now feel calm, content, or even peaceful. It's okay if you still feel upset.

6. Focus your attention on the setback you're experiencing. Acknowledge the situation for what it is, without judging yourself in the process. Notice any tendencies to criticize yourself.

7. Consider what expectations you had for this situation. Reflect on your desire to control the outcome. See if you can let go, even slightly, of any expectations you had before this setback about how you would achieve what you wanted.

8. Next, imagine picking yourself back up and standing tall again after being knocked down by this temporary defeat. See yourself confident enough to move forward from this disappointment. Envision yourself determined and excited to try again.

9. Then, envision yourself working toward a big win. See yourself giving it your all, with passion and faith that things will work out the way they're meant to.

10. See yourself overcoming this current disappointment and winning. Feel the joy of finally achieving your goal. Imagine what else you might feel when you finally have that big win.

11. Finally, while you may strive to win, remind yourself that your worth is not based on winning or achieving. Be proud of the fact that you gave your best effort and worked hard toward your goal. And know that your win is not your identity. Self-compassion is about having the confidence to keep trying to win and loving yourself regardless.

12. End your visualization by refocusing on relaxing your entire body and taking another 10 deep belly breaths.

10 Use Your Superpowers

TIME: 10 minutes
BEST FOR: Coping with stressful life events

When stressful life events trigger negative emotions, this guided meditation counteracts anxiety, hopelessness, and anger. It connects you with your inner superhero, so you can use your superpowers to overcome life's problems.

Steps

1. This meditation is best done seated cross-legged on a cushion or in a chair. You may find it helpful to play soothing nature sounds in the background, such as gentle rain or ocean noises.

2. Begin by closing your eyes and grounding yourself with five deep breaths. Inhale slowly through your nose for as long as you can, and exhale just as slowly.

3. Next, bring your attention to all your superpowers. Think about your strengths as a person. Consider the times in your life when you felt most successful. Recall times in your life when you overcame difficult circumstances. Think about the knowledge, experience, and abilities that brought you success and got you through tough times. What are some of your strengths in relationships? What are some traits and experiences that make you more resilient?

4. Take another five deep breaths, inhaling slowly as for long as you can and exhaling for just as long.

5. Next, think about how you can use your superpowers to navigate your current life stressor. What personal strengths could benefit you in this situation? How can you apply those strengths in a valuable way?

6. Take another five deep breaths, inhaling slowly as long for as you can and exhaling for just as long.

7. Finally, think about how the life event that's challenging you will help you grow as a person. How will surviving this situation build your character? What new superpowers might you develop as you persevere through this stressful life event?

8. Take another five deep breaths, inhaling slowly as long as you can and exhaling just as long.

9. End by asking yourself, "Is there space to not only survive this life event, but to also thrive in the process?" Envision yourself not only making it through this difficult situation but using all your superpowers to thrive with joy and passion.

11 Silver Lining

TIME: 10 minutes
BEST FOR: Coping with sadness and depression

When we're sad or depressed, it can be difficult to allow any other emotions into our experience. However, it is possible to feel joy even when in emotional pain. The goal of this exercise is not to avoid or try to get rid of your sadness, but to allow yourself to feel other emotions as well. If you continuously choose to feel joy every day, your sadness can diminish or even go away completely. Use the exercise below to build moments of love, peace, and compassion into your daily routine, especially when you feel overwhelmed by emotional pain. I suggest conducting it at the beginning of the day, if possible.

Steps

1. **Self-care.** Plan to add self-care into your day. How can you take care of yourself today? Perhaps you can plan a relaxing bubble bath or set aside 15 minutes to read a book with a cup of hot tea. Other options include yoga, exercise, eating a healthy meal, getting a massage, doing an at-home facial, or taking a nap. Whatever the activity, it should bring you a feeling of peace, relaxation, or calmness.

2. **Self-compassion.** Plan to add self-compassion into your day. You can set an intention to be patient with yourself all day or to use a self-compassion mantra, such as "I offer myself kindness no matter what," throughout the day. Or plan to spend time on any of the self-compassion exercises within this book, choosing a favorite that brings you a sense of love and comfort.

3. **Pleasure.** Schedule something fun that can make you feel excited and joyful, even if you're not feeling that way right now. It might be streaming your favorite television show or having coffee with a friend. Maybe it's reconnecting with a hobby, like gardening or cooking. You might spend time fully present with your family or enjoy the sights and sounds of nature at a park or on a walking trail.

4. **Appreciation.** Plan to take some time to appreciate life. You might pause at a designated time of day to reflect on everything you're thankful for. Or develop a more formal daily gratitude practice, such as writing down 10 things you're grateful for at bedtime every night.

5. **Mindfulness practice.** Plan to spend time today practicing mindfulness with one or more of the exercises in this book. Consider setting a consistent time each day for a mindfulness exercise, such as meditating each morning.

12 Peace in a Box

TIME: 15 minutes

BEST FOR: Feeling overwhelmed, anxious, or stressed

Our senses have a potent effect on how we feel. In this exercise, you'll leverage that power by gathering objects that will soothe you when you feel overwhelmed, anxious, or stressed. You'll craft an emergency kit containing self-soothing elements that appeal to all five senses, which you can keep handy and access in the moment whenever strong negative emotions take hold.

Steps

1. Choose a small box or bag to hold your self-soothing kit. Almost any container can work; be sure it fits the space where you'll keep it. If you'll want to access it at work, for example, it may need to fit in a drawer or locker. You may want to craft multiple kits so you can keep one at home, one at the office, one in your car, and so on.

2. Use the following categories, representing the five senses, to add items to your kit. Choose at least one object for each category. Be sure to select items that you personally find soothing and that stimulate feelings of self-compassion. Use the suggestions below to get started, but be as creative as you like. You can add to the kit as new ideas strike you.

   ◇ SIGHT. Choose objects that you find pleasing to the eye. Examples include a calming picture of the beach, funny comic strips, a picture of a loved one, or a postcard or clipping that displays a favorite work of art. Another idea is to add a picture of yourself during a happy occasion, perhaps with friends or family. You may also include self-written mantra cards, with self-compassion affirmations and words of encouragement.

◇ SOUND. Add things that are comforting and pleasant to your sense of sound. Possibilities include a sound bowl, a small music box, or a list of favorite songs to play on your phone.

◇ TOUCH. Add items that you find relaxing to touch. Examples include a swatch of soft fabric, a feather, a fidget toy, some silly putty, or a stress ball. You might include massage oil to give yourself a hand massage (see the exercise on page 94) or mala beads to use while meditating.

◇ TASTE. Add items that are soothing to your palate, something with a taste that you enjoy. Ideas include a small piece of chocolate, mints, chewing gum, taffy, or a chamomile tea bag.

◇ SMELL. Add your favorite scented items. Examples include an aromatherapy candle, incense, essential oils, scented lotion, or dried flowers.

13 Focus on the Journey

TIME: 5–10 minutes

BEST FOR: Feeling unmotivated, getting inspired

Why do we sometimes feel unmotivated, even when the goal we want to reach is important to us? Often it's because we can't detach our sense of self-worth from the end goal. We feel as if failure will define us, and the fear that comes with that kind of pressure makes it difficult to move forward. This meditation deflates that fear by reminding you that your true self is not defined by failure or success. Freed by self-compassion, you'll summon your inner will and be inspired to act. This exercise uses a breathing technique called "skull shining breath" to give you energy. (The name is a translation from Sanskrit, with a connotation similar to clearing one's head.)

Steps

1. Find a comfortable and quiet space for meditation. Take a seated position on a cushion with legs crossed or sit comfortably in a chair. Relax your shoulders and arms, and place both hands on your abdomen, one on top of the other.

2. Start this meditation using skull shining breathing: Take a long slow inhale through your nose, sending air to your lower abdomen. Feel your hands rise as you inhale.

3. Next, expel 10 forceful exhales through your nose. With each exhalation, contract your lower abdomen inward while you press your hands inward as well.

4. Repeat this breathing for 10 cycles. Then, take three deep cleansing breaths before gently coming back to normal breathing.

5. Shift your attention to just watching your breath. Observe each inhale and exhale for about a minute.

6. Next, focus your thoughts on why you're in need of motivation; that is, the task or action that you need to perform. Recall why you want to get this task done. Repeat your reason three times in your mind.

7. Visualize yourself summoning your willpower and becoming highly motivated. Imagine what it feels like to be excited by and dedicated to this task, as if you want to do nothing else. Say to yourself, "I have what it takes to work toward my goal." Repeat this statement in your mind three times.

8. Now remind yourself that your value is not contingent on achievement. Say to yourself, "I am proud of my intention to work toward my goal, regardless of the outcome." Repeat this in your mind three times.

9. Finally, reflect on the fact that regardless of the outcome, showing up to take your shot, with passion, is the most important factor. There's no success if you don't try. Say to yourself, "It's about the journey, not the destination." Repeat this three times.

10. Finish this meditation with 10 more cycles of skull shining breath. Then follow this breathing with three deep cleansing breaths.

14 Me First

TIME: 15 minutes

BEST FOR: People pleasers, role strain, feeling burned out

Managing your emotions is particularly difficult if you're feeling burned out. A state of burnout can result from having too many roles in life, from expending too much energy on people-pleasing, or from exhausting work demands and other external factors. This mindful writing exercise will help you avoid or escape burnout by teaching you to prioritize your own needs, a central tenet of self-compassion. Remember, you can't live up to your commitments or offer help to others if you're not tending to your own well-being.

Steps

1. You will need a blank sheet of paper and a pen or pencil for this activity or a digital drawing tool that you're familiar with.

2. Start by drawing a medium-size circle in the center of the page.

3. Divide the page into four quadrants or squares, two above and two below, with the circle at the center.

4. Use the circle to set your intention for this practice. Write the following mantra, or create one of your own, in the center circle: "I deserve space to cultivate happiness for myself."

5. In the upper left quadrant, list all the reasons you think you're burned out. Think about how you came to feel this way and what's contributing to feeling so strained and overextended.

6. Use the upper right quadrant to reflect on boundaries. Write about how you can instill healthy
   boundaries to protect your time, space, energy, and
   other resources. For example, you might turn off your
   phone for a block of time every day or create an email
   auto-response stating that nonurgent messages might
   not be answered right away.

7. In the lower left quadrant, describe a daily ritual you
   can realistically implement to take care of yourself.
   Include what time of day you will do this and your
   plan for gathering whatever you will need to make
   this happen. Your ritual could be as simple as a cup
   of tea, a warm bath, or a walk through the neigh-
   borhood while listening to music. Or choose one of
   the exercises in this book that you find particularly
   healing.

8. Last, in the final lower right quadrant, reflect on how
   you would like to feel going forward. Write down
   emotions that you would like to experience once your
   burnout has lifted. Then, add some activities that can
   help you feel these emotions.

9. Once you have completed this exercise, keep this page
   in a prominent location to remind you to put yourself first.

REFLECTION ONE

Many difficult emotions stem from our judgmental inner critic. As negative as that voice can be, we usually develop this self-critic to protect ourselves. In your journal, reflect on how you developed your own self-critic and consider the deeper purpose it serves. How does that voice affect your thinking and emotions? What is it protecting you from? For example, you might start by writing, "My inner critic keeps me from making connections with other people. Its deeper purpose is to protect me from rejection."

REFLECTION TWO

Refer to the journal prompt on the previous page and recall the deeper purpose of your inner critic. Now use that information to create your inner "bestie," a friendly, encouraging inner voice. In this new voice, write down some advice to yourself that will fulfill the purpose of your critic, but in a loving way. For instance, if your inner critic served to protect you from disappointment by discouraging you from taking chances, your inner bestie might remind you that disappointment won't crush you, and that you can learn from it and try again.

Self-love is respecting my
beautiful body. Yes, it is beautiful.
It was divinely designed
especially for me. A sacred
creation of self-knowledge
which brings me limitless
opportunities to experience
myself in the moment.

—MICHELLE MARIE McGRATH

Chapter 4

BEFRIENDING YOUR BODY

Introduction

Each of us gets only one body, so naturally the relationship with our physical being plays a huge role in our ability to live a fulfilling life. But we're all bombarded with continuous messages telling us to conform to perfect standards of beauty. And our busy lifestyles can reduce the self-care that keeps our bodies healthy to a minimum. This makes self-compassion for our bodies an essential tool for existing in the modern world. Without it, we're vulnerable to negative feelings about our physical selves, and we let our physical health fall by the wayside. With it, we can develop a healthier concept of self, gain freedom to accept ourselves beyond external validations about our physical traits, and resist pressures to fit an ideal body type. Self-compassion ushers in the acceptance, love, and sense of responsibility to care for our bodies that can transform the way we feel about ourselves.

The goal of this book is to give you a well-rounded strategy of mindfulness to cultivate self-compassion. In previous chapters, we addressed the mind with attention to our thoughts and approached the spirit with attention to our emotions. Now it's time to complete the mind-spirit-body connection. The exercises in this chapter are not intended to change your body to fit an ideal standard or give you an excuse to neglect taking care of your body. Rather, these mindfulness techniques will help you feel at home in your own skin, celebrate your body, and develop habits that promote lasting physical vitality.

Two aspects of self-compassion that are particularly important for improving physical health are self-awareness and self-care. You'll come across these concepts again and again in the following pages. By becoming more aware of our bodies, we empower ourselves to accept how we look, to love our physicality, and to feel grounded in our bodies instead of shamed or awkward. And when we hone our ability to care for our bodies, we not only reap the benefits of greater physical health, we gift ourselves with self-kindness that's an antidote to stress and negativity.

This chapter will enable you to develop new ways to connect with your body, empowering you to direct the six principles of self-compassion to your physical side, as well as to your thoughts and emotions. As you use the exercises in this chapter to improve your relationship with your physical self, take stock of how you view your body and how you treat it. For added success, use your journal to keep track of which exercises resonate with you the most, and continue to write down how each exercise makes you feel and any thoughts that arise.

Shame Buster

TIME: 10 minutes
BEST FOR: Overcoming body shame

If you have painful thoughts and feelings about your body, you're not alone. It can be so hard to avoid comparing ourselves to the unrealistic images that we see in advertising and entertainment media. In this exercise, you'll learn a mindful drawing technique that will raise your awareness of the shame you experience related to your body and help you move toward self-acceptance with a meditation to cope with that identified shame.

Steps

1. Gather materials: you'll need paper, a pen, colored pencils, markers, or crayons.

2. Draw a rudimentary outline of your body, with your head, neck, shoulders, chest, torso, hips, legs, and feet clearly defined. Don't worry about the quality of your drawing.

3. Close your eyes. Think about which parts of your body you're most critical of, ashamed of, or feel disconnected from.

4. Once you have these body parts in mind, open your eyes and shade in those areas of your outline, using a color that best symbolizes what the shame feels like.

5. Close your eyes once more. Think about times in your life when you felt ashamed for any reason. In these situations, what did you look like when you experienced shame? What sensations in your body do you feel when you experience shame? Do you slump your shoulders, frown, or have sweaty palms?

6. Once you're aware of how you experience shame in your body, open your eyes and color in those areas of your body drawing.

7. Now, take a moment to study your outline. Notice the areas of your body that you feel ashamed about and the body sensations you feel when you experience shame.

8. Close your eyes and focus on your breathing, taking slow and controlled inhales and exhales.

9. Say this mantra in your head as you breathe: "I accept my body and release all tension caused by shame."

10. Inhale slowly and imagine breathing into the designated body space with healing breath. As you exhale, imagine sending healing breath to a body part that you identified above.

11. Slowly exhale and move on to the next body part that you identified.

12. When you have sent loving breath to all body parts identified, return to slow breathing and repeat the mantra "I accept my body and release all tension caused by shame."

13. Gently release control of your breath, return to normal breathing, and open your eyes when you are ready.

2 Wrapped in Love

TIME: 15 minutes
BEST FOR: Cultivating self-love and body positivity

Loving your body requires body awareness, the feeling of being grounded in your body, and a conscious effort to offer kindness to your physical self. Develop those qualities with this mindful body scan, which brings warm self-compassion from head to toe.

Steps

1. Find a comfortable position, seated or lying down, and close your eyes.

2. Slowly inhale through your nose and imagine sending your breath through your body all the way down to your toes. On the exhale, slowly send your breath back up from your toes all the way up your body and back out through your mouth.

3. Take 10 sets of breaths this way.

4. Gently return to normal breathing.

5. Imagine a ball of bright white light hovering above your head. This light represents consciousness and self-awareness.

6. Visualize this white light descending and beginning to wash over you. Try to relax each body part that the light touches as it flows down your body.

7. Imagine the light coming down the crown of your head, flowing down your forehead and the back of your head. Feel the light as it continues down your eyes, nose, and mouth. Feel your jaw relax and notice the back of your head relaxing.

8. Allow this white conscious light to continue slowly streaming down the front and back of your body. Feel your muscles sequentially relax as the light streams down your neck, arms, and shoulders; your chest, back, and abdomen; your hips, knees, calves, ankles, feet, and toes.

9. Once the light reaches your toes, imagine the glow changing to a warm red ball of energy beneath the soles of your feet. This energy represents warmth, love, and acceptance.

10. Take 10 additional cleansing breaths, sending your breath down to your toes as you inhale, and back up and out on the exhales.

11. Imagine the red energy beginning to slowly permeate up your body. Without rushing, see and feel the red energy coming up your toes, ankles and calves; your knees, thighs, and hips; your abdomen, back and chest; your shoulders, arms, neck, and head.

12. Once the loving energy reaches the crown of your head, take one minute to imagine your whole body relaxed and wrapped in warm love before opening your eyes.

3 A Handful of Bliss

TIME: 10 minutes
BEST FOR: Reducing stress and tension

Finding ways to release the tension in our bodies is an excellent form of self-care. This exercise builds self-compassion by teaching you an easy and effective self-massage. Hand massage has been shown to reduce stress and anxiety, boost mood, and improve sleep; give yourself this kind gift whenever you need it.

Steps

1. A warm towel, massage oil, or your favorite scented lotion can enhance this exercise, but the result is just as effective without them. Start the process by setting an intention to stay mindfully present throughout this exercise. As you massage each hand, breathe slowly and try to observe each physical sensation.

2. If a warm towel is available, wrap your left hand with it for one minute to help relax your muscles.

3. If using oil or lotion, remove your hand from the towel and apply massage oil or lotion to your left hand. Add oil or lotion to the palm and fingertips of your right hand.

4. Place your left hand into your right hand, with your right thumb on your left palm, and your right fingers supporting your left hand from underneath.

5. Using moderate pressure and small circular motions (about the width of a dime), massage your left palm with your right thumb. Move your thumb clockwise, slowly expanding the circle until your whole palm relaxes.

6. Now move your thumb in smooth, longer strokes, rubbing your thumb from the base of the palm to the tip of each finger in turn, keeping moderate pressure.

7. Next, use your right index finger and right thumb to lightly squeeze your palm between your index and middle fingers. Massage that area with your thumb on the palm side, in a small circular motion. Repeat between the other fingers in turn.

8. Hold your left pinky between the base of the palm and the first knuckle of the finger using your right thumb and index finger, with your thumb on the palm side. Gently press, making a circular motion with your thumb. Move up the finger, massaging between the knuckles. Repeat for the other left-hand fingers and thumb.

9. Turn the left hand over and use your right thumb to gently massage the webbing between each finger, again moving in a circular motion.

10. Repeat the entire process on your right hand. Warm your hand with a towel, if available, and add oil or lotion if desired.

Just Relax

TIME: 15 minutes

BEST FOR: Relaxation and reducing stress

Relaxing isn't always easy; it can be hard for us to release the stress we carry. Here's a progressive muscle relaxation technique that uses mindfulness to familiarize your body with the sensation of letting go. For this exercise, you will gently tense and relax your muscles. If you're unsure whether you should practice this exercise because of health issues, please check with your doctor first.

Steps

1. Sit comfortably in a chair.

2. For each area listed, inhale slowly for five seconds while tensing that muscle group. Then slowly release the tension and relax that muscle group while you exhale slowly for five seconds. Pause to let the tension fade, and return to a comfortable posture, then move on. Pay close attention to the sensation of your muscles relaxing. Be sure to use the breathing technique to time your movements.

   ◇ FEET. Begin by tensing both feet. Extend your legs in front of you so your feet are off the floor. Then flex your feet, pulling the tops of your feet toward you and curling your toes as you inhale (five seconds), then relaxing them as you exhale (five seconds).

   ◇ CALVES. Tense your calves by lifting your heels off the floor and tightening your calf muscles, then relax.

   ◇ THIGHS. Extend your legs out in front of you and squeeze your thigh muscles, then relax.

◇ STOMACH. Suck in your stomach muscles and clench your abdomen, then relax.

◇ CHEST. Take an even deeper inhalation while pushing out your chest, feeling the breath push against your chest, then relax.

◇ BACK. Arch your back while contracting your back muscles. Feel the small of your back tighten, and then relax.

◇ SHOULDERS. Lift your shoulders up toward your ears, then relax.

◇ NECK. Lower your chin to your chest, feeling the back of your neck tightening, then relax.

◇ ARMS AND HANDS. Stretch both arms out to your sides, holding them parallel to the floor and stretching them as far as they'll go, and clench your fists. Then relax.

◇ MOUTH AND JAW. Make the most exaggerated smile you can, with teeth showing and clenched together. Then relax.

◇ EYES. Squeeze your eyelids shut, then open them.

◇ FOREHEAD. Scrunch the muscles in forehead by raising your eyebrows, then relax.

3. End by taking a deep inhalation and slowly exhaling as you let your whole body relax.

Bath Time Oasis

TIME: 30 minutes

BEST FOR: Detoxing the body and decompressing

If you lead a busy lifestyle, it may be difficult to find time to relax. But a tranquil bath doesn't require much planning and can become an easy method to foster self-compassion for your body as you unwind and decompress. Adding mindfulness to the mix creates a bath time oasis that will immerse you in self-kindness and self-care.

Steps

1. Start this practice by setting an intention to cleanse your mind and reset your mood. Recite a self-affirming mantra, such as "I deserve to decompress and pamper my body," to seal your intention.

2. While you fill your bathtub with warm water, sit next to the tub and practice deep breathing as you listen to the running water.

3. While in the bathtub, focus your thoughts on the relaxing sensations, from the warmth of the water to the feeling of tension leaving your body.

4. Consider using any of the following for an added element of self-love:

   ◇ BATH SALTS. Epsom salt or Himalayan pink salt contains minerals said to help detox the skin and relax tired muscles.

◇ CRYSTALS. Many people rave about their healing power. Whether you're a believer or not, putting crystals around the tub can add a soothing aesthetic to help you relax.

◇ AROMATHERAPY. Try using an essential oil diffuser to add a calming scent, such as lavender, to your bath experience. The sensation will help you stay present during this exercise.

◇ CANDLES AND DIM LIGHTS. Create a tranquil spa-like experience with dim lights, and place candles in safe places around your tub to help produce the perfect ambience. Lowered light will also prepare your body and mind for sleep.

◇ BUBBLE BATH. Bubbles just may be the quintessential bath accessory, and a bubble bath can be very moisturizing for your skin as well as a fun sensory indulgence. If you aren't into bubbles, try a bath tea product to treat your skin without the suds.

◇ MUSIC. Play calming music, nature sounds, or your favorite mellow playlist. This will help you tune out distractions and stay in the moment.

◇ HOT TEA. Indulge in a hot cup of herbal tea as you bathe to help soothe your nervous system.

◇ WARM ROBE AND TOWEL. Before starting your bath, put a bathrobe and towel in the dryer for 30 minutes. Place them near the tub and use them to dry off after. The warm sensation will be a perfect peaceful ending to your bath ritual.

6 Day of Compassion

TIME: One day
BEST FOR: Promoting physical health and vitality

Ayurveda is an ancient healing system that originated in India and is still practiced today to improve quality of life and vitality. A mindful approach to living that aims to balance the mind, body, and spirit, Ayurveda has much to offer for increasing self-compassion. This exercise incorporates Ayurvedic concepts into a day routine that you can use to practice self-care, rebalance your body chemistry, boost energy, and offer your body kindness. Try to integrate these practices into your schedule whenever you can.

Steps

1. **Waking.** Aim to wake up before sunrise. Upon waking, drink a large glass of warm lemon water to start your day hydrated (juice from half a lemon in eight ounces of water is a good ratio to try). Take time to empty your bladder and colon before beginning the day's activities, as a way of eliminating toxins and rehydrating your tissues. After brushing your teeth, gently scrape your tongue with a tongue cleaner to help remove bacteria, enhance your sense of taste, and generally improve your overall health.

2. **Morning.** In Ayurvedic traditions, the morning is the most peaceful time of the day. Use this time for meditation or any favorite mindfulness practice from this book. After clearing your mind, engage in a self-massage (see A Handful of Bliss, page 94) to further cultivate peace before your day begins. Eat a light breakfast, preferably before 8 a.m.

3. **Midday.** Use midday to get the bulk of your work done. Ayurveda dictates the most productive hours of the day are between 10 a.m. and 2 p.m. At noon, have a healthy meal. Lunch should be the largest meal of your day. Go for a walk to help with digestion and to reduce tension and stress.

4. **Evening.** Exercise between 5 p.m. and 6 p.m. Eat a light, healthy dinner before 8 p.m. Be mindful as you savor your dinner, and disconnect from your phone, TV, and work. End the evening with a relaxing bath (see Bath Time Oasis, page 98).

5. **Bedtime.** Write in your journal, describing what you're grateful for. Spend time relaxing for at least 30 minutes before you go to sleep. Some ideas for bedtime relaxation include meditation, drinking hot tea, reading a book, or practicing a mindful body scan (see Wrapped in Love, page 92). Aim to fall asleep by 10 p.m. To improve sleep, turn off all electronics and darken your bedroom as much as possible.

Giving Thanks

TIME: 15 minutes
BEST FOR: Increasing body positivity

Self-compassion can create greater appreciation for your body. This writing exercise is a technique you can use to help cultivate positive thoughts related to your physical self and practice self-love toward it. Record your insights in your journal, and review when you're feeling negative about your body.

Steps

1. Find a quiet and comfortable space for writing.

2. Start with a grounding visualization: Set a timer for five minutes. Close your eyes and bring your attention to your breath. As you observe each inhalation and exhalation, notice any sensations you feel in your body. What parts feel calm, relaxed, and comfortable? Where do you feel tension, pain, or discomfort?

3. Refocus on your breath. Inhale through your nose and imagine sending breath to every part of your body, from head to toe. On the exhale, imagine retracting this breath from your entire body and out through your mouth. Continue until your timer sounds.

4. Open your eyes and begin to reflect on your body's strengths.

5. As you reflect, write down all the things about your body for which you're grateful. Here are some pointers:

+ Write freely, recording whatever comes to mind, and try not to get stuck analyzing your body.

+ Think of ways in which your body allows you to function in life.

+ Think of ways that your body is strong or flexible.

+ Reflect on ways that your body has healed from illness and injury or survived damaging events.

+ Consider your physical health, and how your body has sustained life for you.

+ Think about the large and small miracles of the human body: the uniqueness of fingerprints, the ability to birth children, even your beating heart, ceaselessly working to keep you alive.

+ If your mind strays to self-criticism, gently acknowledge that your attention has strayed, and refocus on appreciating your body.

6. Spend about 10 minutes creating this list. When you're done, end by taking a moment to notice how you feel emotionally. Take a deep breath in, and on the out breath, say to yourself, "I appreciate my body."

Laugh Out Loud

TIME: 10 minutes
BEST FOR: Cultivating joy

Laughter is said to be good for the soul. It's a unique human capability that speaks directly to the mind-body connection. As a form of self-compassion, laughter is a great way to use our bodies to improve our mood. This exercise teaches you how to use "laughter meditation," conscious laughter, as an offer of self-kindness that promotes feelings of joy. Use this mindful laughter meditation anytime to pause, connect to the present, and take a joyful break. And enjoy practicing a form of meditation that's very different from what you're used to!

Steps

1. **Warm up.** Begin this exercise by warming up your face with the following gentle stretches. Cycle through them for three minutes, holding each stretch for a moment before slowly relaxing.

    + **Face scrunch.** Scrunch all your facial muscles together by squeezing your eyes closed and puckering your lips up toward your nose. Hold for three seconds and relax.

    + **Open mouth.** Open your mouth as wide as you can three times.

    + **Mouth circles.** Pucker your lips while moving them in circles to the left and then to the right.

    + **Big smile.** Smile as big as you can three times.

2. **Laugh!** Start the laughing process by smiling as you breathe deeply. Close your eyes and envision yourself laughing, with your most authentic, uninhibited laugh in response to something completely hilarious. You don't have to have the funny thing in mind, just imagine yourself laughing hysterically. Allow your smile to get bigger. Turn your smile into a small chuckle. After about a minute of smiling and chuckling, advance to full-blown laughing for about four minutes. Initially, you will feel like you are forcing laughter, but don't worry. After a short while, it will feel more genuine, and you'll be surprised how strong your impulse to laugh can be. Engage your face muscles and try to produce a laugh that resonates from your belly.

3. **Reflect.** Once you stop laughing, take a few seconds to regain composure. Then reflect on the following:

   ✦ Were you able to stay present as you laughed?

   ✦ Did you notice any emotions arise as you laughed?

   ✦ Did you find it difficult to let yourself laugh and have a bit of carefree fun?

   ✦ Did you judge yourself in any way during the meditation?

   ✦ Can you take a moment to thank yourself for making time to be present in this lighthearted, joyful way?

My Beating Heart

TIME: 10 minutes

BEST FOR: Managing stress and anxiety

Have you ever felt anxious and noticed your heartbeat racing? An increased heartbeat is a physical byproduct of mental stress, as your body prepares to cope with a threat perceived by your mind. Because of that mind-body connection, however, slowing our heartbeat can diminish our stress and anxiety. This exercise teaches you how to calm your heart rate to relax your mood. Present moment awareness, self-awareness, and self-kindness will help you persevere during a tense situation. This technique uses exercise to raise your heartbeat so you can practice in the absence of actual anxiety. Once you've learned the method, call on it in times of heightened stress.

Steps

1. To practice this exercise when you are not feeling anxious, do jumping jacks for one minute, if your health permits. Please check with your doctor first if you have concerns about increasing your heart rate.

2. Notice how you feel physically. Sit and place your hand over your chest, feeling your heartbeat.

3. Acknowledge how you feel emotionally. Name any anxiety or stress you might be feeling. Remind yourself that this emotion is just a temporary experience. (If you're practicing, you may not be feeling significant anxiety. Label whatever emotion arises.)

4. Practice box breathing for three minutes: Inhale for four seconds, hold your breath for four seconds, exhale for four seconds, then hold for four seconds before starting over.

5. Do some gentle stretching while seated. If the stretches are too difficult, the box breathing and visualization (step 6) will still be helpful.

   + Lift your arms over your head and reach for the sky for 30 seconds.

   + Roll your shoulders backward and forward, five times in each direction.

   + Roll your neck, gently tilting your head to the right and left five times each.

   + Place your hands on your hips, with elbows pointing backward. Slowly tilt your head backward, while arching your back, for 30 seconds.

   + Place your hands on your knees and bow your head. Pull your stomach in while curling your back for 30 seconds.

   + Roll your ankles in circles, spending 30 seconds on each foot.

6. Finish by relaxing your entire body. Imagine sinking into your chair, with all your muscles melting downward. Tell yourself "relax" three times in your head. Sit for two minutes, visualizing yourself becoming completely calm.

7. Place your hand over your chest and feel your heartbeat once more. Notice how much slower it is.

10 Strike a Pose

TIME: 6 minutes

BEST FOR: Increasing confidence, improving mood

Social psychologist and researcher Amy Cuddy has shown that changing our body position can lead to changes in body chemistry, as well as in our emotions. Amazingly, positioning yourself in a way that suggests you're confident or proud generates those feelings inside you. In fact, such power poses are a great way to increase self-confidence, reduce stress, and thwart self-doubt.

Steps

1. Find a private space where you will feel comfortable practicing these power poses.

2. Hold the following poses for two minutes each. A key factor to making these poses beneficial is tapping into the emotions each pose evokes. As you embody each pose, try your hardest to feel the associated emotion. Think of a time that you felt the emotion and allow yourself to feel that way now.

   ◇ **SUPERHERO POSE FOR CONFIDENCE.** Stand with your feet at hip-width apart. Place your hands on your hips, elbows pointing out. Relax your shoulders and hold your chin up. Connect with the feelings of confidence. Stand embodying self-assurance, strength, and courage. Allow this feeling to permeate your whole body as you stand tall, strong, powerful, and ready for anything.

◇ MOUNTAIN POSE FOR CALMNESS. Stand tall, with feet at hip-width apart. Press down on the soles of your feet to make sure you're fully grounded. Stand with your legs straight; tuck your tailbone and straighten your back. Roll your shoulders up, back, then down as you hold your arms down by your side. Relax your jaw muscles and lift the crown of your head to the sky. Embody calmness. Be as steady and unmoving as a mountain. Remind yourself that you're safe and secure, and truly connect with feeling composed.

◇ VICTORY POSE FOR PRIDE. Stand with feet at hip-width apart. Slightly arch your upper back, stick out your chest, and raise your hands to the sky, arms straight up as if you'd just broke through the tape at the finish line of a race. As you hold this pose for two minutes, embody the feeling of pride. Stand in this pose connected to feelings of satisfaction and honor.

3. End by taking a moment to notice your emotions. Observe how changing your body positions changed your mind-set.

Yoga for Your Heart

TIME: 5 minutes

BEST FOR: Cultivating self-love

Yoga and the chakra system arose in ancient India, and they offer much wisdom related to self-compassion. Yoga helps us use our bodies to calm our mind with physical postures. The chakra system helps us understand our hierarchy of emotional needs by describing seven centers of spiritual energy in the body. Traditionally, yoga poses focused on the fourth chakra (said to be located at the level of the heart) are considered useful in fostering self-love. Whether you consider the chakras to be real or metaphorical, try this short yoga sequence to increase self-compassion using the mind-body connection. Hold the poses for one minute each, staying in position as best as you can without straining. Don't hold your breath; intentionally observe each inhalation and exhalation.

Steps

1. **Crossed leg (Sukhasana).** Sit on the floor or an exercise mat with your legs crossed and your palms pressed together in a prayer position in front of your chest. Set an intention to connect with your body without judgment. This pose relaxes the mind and helps decrease anxiety.

2. **Supine plank (Purvottanasana).** Next, extend your legs straight out in front of you; lean back on your hands, with palms against the floor, fingers pointing forward, hands at shoulder width behind you. Point your toes forward, press your

soles to the floor, and push your body upward, rising on your hands and feet. Keeping your legs together, arc your body, and push your chest up. Slowly tilt your head back, with your face toward the sky. This pose symbolizes expressing love to others, and helps you practice opening your heart and offering love.

3. **Seated boat (Paripurna Navasana).** Lower yourself carefully to the ground. Sit with your legs in front of you, knees bent, feet flat on the floor. Place your hands under your knees. Raise your feet and lower legs until your shins are parallel to the floor. Release your grasp, keeping your legs in position, and extend your arms out in front, alongside your legs. Keep your spine straight as you gaze forward. Holding this pose helps cultivate inner strength and perseverance.

4. **Upward-facing dog (Urdhva Mukha Svanasana).** Transition to lying down on your stomach, arms on each side of you, bent in a push-up position, your hands even with your shoulders. Your legs should be together, straight out behind you. Point your toes backward, push down with the tops of your feet and hands, and lift your hips up off the floor. As you push yourself up with your arms, raise your chest up and your head to face forward. Hold the position with your arms straight up and down, tailbone tucked, and try not to overarch your back. This pose is known to reduce feelings of sadness and being overwhelmed.

5. Return to a crossed-leg position, hands in a prayer position at your heart. Remember your intention to connect with your body in a loving way. Take three deep breaths to conclude the practice.

12 TIPPing Point

TIME: 10 minutes
BEST FOR: Calming down

Learning to regulate difficult emotions and calm your-self down is a great way to cultivate the perseverance needed for self-compassion. Dialectical behavioral therapy offers a tool called the TIPP skill to help calm the nervous system in times of distress. This mindful-ness exercise uses it to increase self-compassion. Before trying it, be sure that cooling your body temperature and performing intense exercise at times of distress are approved by your doctor.

Steps

1. Begin by acknowledging how you feel. Boost your self-awareness by closing your eyes and taking stock of what emotions and body sensations you feel in the present moment. Be sure not to judge yourself.

2. Next, set an intention for your practice by saying the following affirmation in your head: "My body has healing powers." Then engage the four TIPP calming tactics:

T: TEMPERATURE. Focus on decreasing your body temperature. There's a reason that "hot" is another word for angry: When we're upset, our temperature usually rises. Taking action to cool down physically helps us tolerate distress. You might place your face in front of an air-conditioning vent, splash cold water on your face, place some ice cubes on the back of your neck, or briefly stick your hands in the freezer.

I: INTENSE EXERCISE. We can use the body to process difficult emotions by engaging in exercise that helps us blow off steam. Some quick activity, such as taking a run down the street, climbing a flight of stairs, vigorously cleaning, or doing jumping jacks, will pump more oxygen to the brain, which reduces stress.

P: PACED BREATHING. Controlled breathing techniques have been shown to be very effective in reducing emotional distress. Take a few minutes to pace your breathing using the following technique:

+ Inhale deeply and slowly and imagine breathing in warm love that permeates your entire body. Be sure to breathe into your belly, expanding the diaphragm.

+ Hold your breath for four seconds.

+ Release the breath, exhaling slowly as you imagine releasing all your emotional pain as you breathe out.

P: PROGRESSIVE MUSCLE RELAXATION. In the Just Relax exercise on page 96, you learned about progressive muscle relaxation, a great way to release tension and cope with stress. Engage in progressive muscle relaxation now, referring to the exercise if needed. As you relax each muscle group, say in your head, "I release all suffering."

13 Exercise Compassion

TIME: 45 minutes

BEST FOR: Reducing self-criticism while working out

Many people have great intentions to start exercising, but their inner critic sabotages their efforts. From comparisons with others' bodies to judgments about your own physique, going to the gym or working out on your own can bring up a great deal of self-doubt. This mindfulness exercise will help you increase self-compassion, so you can experience the positive feelings that come with improving your physical health. Practice it before your workout and any time you feel doubts about your ability to exercise.

Steps

1. Start by setting a compassionate goal for your workout plan. Instead of focusing on losing weight or changing something that you hate about your body, consider the following exercise goals:

   - Increase strength

   - Connect with my body

   - Improve flexibility

   - Increase vitality

   - Improve physical health

   - Increase endurance

   - Be kind to my body

   - Take care of my body

+ Improve alignment

+ Increase mobility

+ Build a better relationship with my body

+ Reduce stress

+ Release endorphins and improve mood

2. To promote body positivity, focus on self-acceptance. Look in the mirror and repeat the following three affirmations:

   + I accept my body for what it is, and I work out only to enhance my strengths.

   + I love my body for allowing me to exercise and improve my health.

   + I am grateful for the body I have now.

3. Begin the workout routine of your choice. Exercise systems that are particularly helpful for body positivity include yoga, Pilates, and tai chi. Foster self-kindness by taking breaks when you need to and drinking plenty of water.

4. As you work out, do an inner critic check. Monitor your thoughts for any judgments, comparisons, or suggestions to quit. Acknowledge self-critical thoughts, and gently reframe them by reminding yourself of your goal. Repeat the above affirmations in your mind.

5. After completing your workout, reward yourself in a healthy way. Be mindful of self-sabotaging thoughts such as "I just worked out, so I deserve to eat this piece of cake." Instead, reward yourself with something that complements the work you just did, such as grabbing a tasty juice or smoothie with a friend, getting a massage, enjoying the steam room at your gym, or getting a pedicure. However you reward yourself, be sure you're being kind to your body.

14 Step by Step

TIME: 15 minutes
BEST FOR: Reenergizing and reducing stress

Walking has been shown to bring many health benefits, such as improving cardiovascular health and reducing stress. Walking meditation expands on these benefits by adding present moment awareness. This mindful exercise is an excellent tool to help increase self-compassion, as it lets you connect with your senses and is an easy and convenient form of self-care and relaxation.

Steps

1. Start by taking one minute to set an intention. You might intend to connect with your senses, practice being in the present moment, enjoy nature, or relax.

2. Go outside and determine a 15-minute route to walk where you will feel safe and calm.

3. Before you start, take one minute to get in touch with your breath to set a tone of connecting with the present moment. Without controlling your breathing, observe each inhalation and exhalation.

4. Begin walking and stay connected with your breath. Take a normal pace and try to stay mindful of your body as you walk. Notice how each step feels. Experience the sensations of your legs moving. Notice your upper body gliding along as you walk.

5. As you walk, mindful of your body and your breath, shift your attention to what you see. Take note of the colors, landscape, people, animals, and buildings, all without judgment. Return to noticing your breath and body for one minute before moving on to observe what you hear. Become aware of the sound of birds chirping or cars passing by. Focus your attention and see if you can hear anything that you hadn't noticed before.

6. Return to observing your breath and body for one minute. Then, shift your focus to what you smell. Notice the scent of the crisp air, the aromas from any shops or restaurants you pass, or take time to stop and smell any flowers or trees.

7. End the walk by thanking yourself for doing something that helps your mind and body. Offer yourself kindness for taking the time out of your day to relax. Take a moment to feel proud of yourself. Close your eyes and imagine this feeling of pride and self-love resonating through your entire body.

REFLECTION ONE

A poor self-image and neglecting your own self-care can lead to physical problems as well as mental health issues. In your journal, write freely about instances when you've lacked self-compassion for your body in the past. Do you avoid exercise or push yourself until you're sore? Reflect on ways that you could come to appreciate your body and prioritize self-care.

REFLECTION TWO

Feeling connected to your body is integral to a positive body image. Imagine that your body could talk to you. What would it say? Would it chide you, encourage you, thank you? In your journal, write a letter to yourself from the perspective of your body.

You yourself, as much as
anybody in the entire universe,
deserve your love and affection.

—THE BUDDHA

Chapter 5

DAY TO DAY

Introduction

It's time to build on everything you've learned and deepen your progress in practicing mindful self-compassion. With this chapter's set of exercises, you'll be empowered to employ mindful self-compassion for life. I've collected some of my favorite strategies to help you make self-compassion part of your everyday routine, creating a strong and solid foundation of self-love and self-kindness that will support you in everything you do.

The goal of this chapter is to help you make mindful self-compassion second nature, an asset that's always available to help you navigate life's challenges with ease. Practicing these exercises will orient your brain to be instinctively compassionate amid stressful triggers and day-to-day challenges. As you incorporate them into your daily activities, start slowly. Add one routine to your day, then another when the first has become a habit. Continue gradually until every day includes numerous episodes of mindful self-compassion, as many as feels right to you.

I encourage you to continue practicing these exercises regularly. Refer to this book so you can return to techniques that you haven't used in a while or to try something new. Whether you're just starting your practice of mindfulness, building momentum, or returning to it after a hiatus, keep using your journal and take note of the value that mindfulness brings. You may find that the same exercises grant you different benefits at different times in your life.

With mindful self-compassion integrated into your everyday living, see if your days don't seem brighter, your problems smaller, your zest for life grander. I predict that they will. I am excited for you to embark on the final exercises in this book, but before jumping into the exercises for this chapter I would like to give you some information on how to use them for maximum results.

Self-compassion is a practice, and these exercises will help you build the habit of implementing self-compassion throughout your day. I advise you to try all the exercises in this chapter and pick the ones you like the best and feel most comfortable with to practice every day. Try to incorporate them into your daily routine, so that eventually you don't even have to think about them. Having morning, midday, and evening routines will help you tremendously in building the habit of practicing these self-compassion techniques. Self-compassion is not something that we practice once and never have to do again. It is an ongoing mindfulness practice, and these strategies will help you continue on your self-compassion journey by infusing it into your everyday life.

Sunrise Ritual

TIME: 20 minutes
BEST FOR: Starting your day off right

An effective morning routine has the power to begin your day on a high note, setting a tone of self-compassion. Done regularly, it will increase resiliency and positive thinking to carry you through unexpected challenges. Use this mindful morning exercise to kick off your day with self-love, clarity, and energy. The acronym PASS will help you remember the steps.

Steps

P: PRANAYAMA (a yoga term for control of one's breathing). Sit in a comfortable position and begin with 10 minutes of this technique, called alternate nostril breathing, intended to activate both sides of the brain:

* Cover your right nostril with your right thumb, and inhale slowly through your left nostril.

* Uncover the right nostril, while covering the left nostril with your right index finger. Exhale slowly through your right nostril.

* Inhale slowly through your right nostril, while still covering the left nostril.

* Cover your right nostril with your right thumb, remove your right index finger, and exhale slowly out your left nostril.

* Continue breathing in this way until 10 minutes has elapsed.

A: AFFIRMATIONS. Spend 5 minutes reading affirmation cards silently or aloud. Here are some tips for creating them:

- Include self-care mantras such as, "No matter what the day brings, may I love myself through it all."

- Include spiritual wisdom such as a scripture verse or a poem.

- Include favorite inspirational quotes reflecting self-kindness.

S: SEE. Visualize the day ahead. See yourself accomplishing your goals, experiencing joy, and being kind with yourself along the way.

S: STRETCH. Gently repeat the following stretches for 30 seconds each.

- Standing forward bend. Stand tall with your feet at hip-width apart. Raise your hands over your head, slowly bend over at the waist, and stretch to touch your toes. Return to an upright position and repeat.

- Cat cow pose. Lower yourself and lean forward so you're resting on your hands and knees in a tabletop position: arms straight, shoulder-width apart, palms flat on the floor, fingers pointing forward. Your knees should be directly beneath your hips and your shins against the floor. Inhale and curve your spine toward the floor, lowering your belly as your chest and tailbone rise. Tilt your head back and gaze toward the ceiling. Hold for three seconds. Exhale and return to the starting position.

  Inhale and arch your back upward toward the ceiling, like a cat, while lowering your head to gaze at the floor. Hold for three seconds, then exhale and return to the starting position.

- Child's pose. From tabletop position, lower your hips backward, bending at the knees into a kneeling position, then rest your tailbone on your heels. Lean forward, bending at the waist, extending your arms straight in front. Smoothly lower your upper body so that your chest rests on your thighs and your forehead and arms touch the floor. Rest in this position for up to 30 seconds.

2 Compassionate Driver

TIME: 10 minutes
BEST FOR: Driving in peace

Driving can be an unpleasant experience if you're running late and traffic is difficult. But it can also be a great opportunity to practice mindful self-compassion. This practice will help you reduce stress and let go of irritation while behind the wheel. Set aside the first 10 minutes of your drive for this exercise to slow down, tune in, and enjoy the trip. As the exercise becomes familiar, try staying in a mindful state for longer periods of time. Eventually this may become your default mode of driving.

Steps

1. Before starting, take time to ground yourself in the present moment with three deep breaths. Let your entire body relax on each exhalation.

2. Set an intention for a peaceful and safe drive. Then engage in your normal safety precautions, such as buckling your seat belt and checking your mirrors.

3. Eliminate distractions like the radio and your phone. Focus your attention on the sensations of driving: what do you see, hear, and feel? Notice what vehicles you see around you, the flow of traffic, the change in vibrations as your wheels cross different surfaces. Feel the air-conditioning or wind on your skin. Notice the landscape, the streetlights, the colors of road signs, and foliage. Take in everything that you are experiencing,

and see if you observe things you missed when taking this route on other occasions.

4. Be mindful to stick to the present. Use stop signs and red lights as reminders to return to the present moment. When you notice your thoughts have strayed, simply acknowledge them, let them go, and refocus your attention on driving.

5. As you drive, notice your own attitudes and thoughts. Notice how your body feels in the seat, how your hands feel on the steering wheel. Also notice your own demeanor. Are you rushing? Do you feel tense or worried? Can you take a moment to slow down and let go of the pressure to hurry?

6. Lastly, savor your time in the car, momentarily disconnected from outside distractions. Take a moment to appreciate the peace that comes with driving in silence. Be grateful for the opportunity to be present. Tune into the blessing that it is to be able to drive. Allow gratitude to transform your trip or daily commute.

3 Mindfulness on the Job

TIME: 10 minutes
BEST FOR: Rejuvenation throughout your workday

Whatever your vocation, you probably experience all sorts of stressors, from deadlines to a heavy workload to various distractions. When a difficult workday calls for an infusion of self-compassion and rejuvenation, this exercise can help. It's a variation on the Pomodoro Technique, a time-management method created by corporate consultant and author Francesco Cirillo. This version will help you take self-compassion breaks to improve your efficiency as you work, so you'll feel rejuvenated and supported.

Steps

1. Divide every work hour into 50 minutes of working, followed by a 10-minute self-compassion break.

2. Use the following strategies during your breaks. Try to take seven breaks a day. Cycle through all the activities, or just the ones you prefer, in whatever order you like.

   ◇ ENERGIZING BREATHING. Spend three minutes simply observing your natural inhalations and exhalations. Then, spend about seven minutes engaging in a breathing technique called Ujjayi Pranayama (which means "victorious lengthening of the breath"). Inhale deeply through your nose, then exhale slowly through your mouth as you constrict your throat and make a "hah" sound.

◇ GET CREATIVE. Use the time for a short creative activity, something you enjoy doing. See Creative Juices, page 144.

◇ CHAIR STRETCHES. Release tension with this easy chair stretch sequence. Start with two minutes of deep breathing. Then spend two minutes each on the following stretches:

1. Reach to the sky: Raise your arms straight up above your head and reach for the sky. Sway both arms to the left and right, then lower them to your sides and repeat.

2. Arm stretch: Bring one arm across your chest while gently pulling at the elbow with the opposite hand. Repeat on the opposite side.

3. Neck rolls: Tuck your chin and slowly, gently roll your head in a circular motion, first to the left, then to the right.

4. Calf raises: Stand behind your chair and place your hands on the top of it to steady yourself. You may need to use a more stable surface if your chair is on wheels. Raise yourself onto the balls of your feet, lifting your heels off the floor and tightening your calf muscles. Hold for a moment and gently lower yourself, then repeat.

◇ HOT TEA AND SNACK. Savor a nice cup of hot tea and your favorite healthy snack, like a piece of fruit.

◇ MINDFUL WALK. Treat yourself to some fresh air and movement. See Step by Step, page 116.

◇ ORGANIZE YOUR WORK SPACE. Clear your mind by tidying up your desktop, cubicle, work space, or locker.

◇ MOTIVATE WITH MUSIC. Create a motivational playlist of songs that bring you pleasure and make you feel energized.

Eating with Compassion

TIME: 30 minutes
BEST FOR: Making the most out of your lunch break

Mindful eating can transform any ordinary meal into an opportunity for joy, relaxation, and gratitude. This mindful eating technique is an excellent tool for self-compassion, as research has shown mindful eating reduces stress, eases digestion, and diminishes food cravings.

Steps

1. Put away distractions, like your phone or paperwork. Enjoy your meal in a location away from your work space. Choose not to multitask. Focus only on eating.

2. Before beginning to eat, take a moment to appreciate your food. Be grateful for having access to this food and its nutrients.

3. Set an intention to focus on what you're experiencing in each moment.

4. Begin by noticing what you see on your plate. Focus on the colors and shapes of your food and take note of what ingredients you can see.

5. Move on to savoring the taste of your food. Pay attention to the flavors in each mouthful. Can you taste the various ingredients? Search for the basic flavor types: sweet, salty, sour, bitter, umami (savory).

6. Notice the texture of your food as you eat. Perceive how your food feels in your mouth as you chew, the sensations against your tongue, teeth, and palate.

7. Take note of the aroma. What scents are strongest? How do they change as the meal progresses?

8. Focus on how it feels to eat in the present moment. Pay attention to the movement of your jaw and tongue. Notice the sensations of cutting your food and put it in your mouth.

9. As you eat, remind yourself to do so slowly and chew thoroughly. Thwart any desire to rush.

10. Continue eating mindfully and consider the origin of your food. Think about the process of how your food was grown and eventually made it to your plate.

11. Stay with observing the present moment, and notice any distracting thoughts, emotions, or sensations that arise. Gently acknowledge any distractions and refocus on eating.

12. As you continue eating, pay attention to your body signals. Can you feel your stomach becoming full, your appetite waning? Tune in to cues of fullness and try not to overeat.

13. When you're done, end by briefly closing your eyes and becoming aware of how you feel. Notice any body sensations present as well as any emotions that arose during the meal.

Family First

TIME: 30 minutes
BEST FOR: Quality time with your family

Nurturing your close relationships is an important aspect of self-compassion. Going through life's daily motions, we sometimes take for granted how special everyday moments spent with our family can be. Putting family first sounds great, but unless we are intentional about it, these moments can easily pass us by. Connect in meaningful ways with those you love the most by developing a daily opportunity to be present with them.

Steps

Choose a designated time when everyone can spend at least 30 minutes of mindful time together. Be patient in negotiating this; you don't want anyone to feel coerced. Follow these principles during family time and allow yourself to truly feel loved in the process.

1. **Be fully attentive.** Aim to give your full focus to interacting with your family. Everyone should put their phones away and engage in an activity that doesn't involve screen time—playing board games, going on a family walk, or cooking together.

2. **Be open.** Keep in mind that your loved ones may be experiencing different emotional states. Be open to accepting them as they come.

3. **Be intentional**. Before family time starts, set an intention to spend mindful quality time with your family. Pausing to remind yourself to be in the moment will help you set the tone for the interaction. See if you can get your family members on board with this intention as well.

4. **Express gratitude**. Acknowledge what you appreciate about your loved ones, saying so out loud.

5. **Cultivate self-awareness**. What feelings arise as you spend time with your family? Recognize feelings of love and joy and let them sink in; experience those feelings washing over your entire body like warm energy. If negative feelings like frustration or impatience arise, acknowledge them and let them go.

6. **Return to the present**. When you become distracted, bring yourself back to focusing on the present moment. Say to yourself, "Right now is family time. I can think about that later."

7. **Seek out micro-moments**. Outside of your designated family time, be alert for smaller moments to savor. Pause when you notice moments of joy, and become the observer as you interact with your family. Notice things about your family you might normally take for granted. Take a moment to express love.

6 Mindfully Social

TIME: 15 minutes

BEST FOR: Using social media in a healthy manner

Many of us use social media daily. While there are many benefits—connecting with others, learning about diverse people and places—there are also many downsides, like increased anxiety, guilt, and envy. This mindfulness exercise will help you develop healthy, mindful social media habits.

Steps

1. Start by limiting your time on social media. Decide on an overall time limit for your daily use, as well as a limit to how long each session lasts. I suggest keeping daily social media access to less than one hour, spending no more than 15 minutes each time.

2. Before viewing any social media feed, pause to be clear about your intention. Remind yourself that you're engaging to connect with friends or take a break and treat yourself to some entertainment. This will help you refrain from mindless scrolling. Before you post or reply, ask yourself, "What do I hope to achieve by posting this content?" Decide if that goal aligns with your values or your true self.

3. Pause before you begin scrolling. Take a deep breath and become fully aware of what you are doing. This will help break the habit of immediately going to social media every time you open your phone.

4. As you view other people's posts, try not to compare yourself to others or judge them. Review the posts with compassion, understanding, and openness for yourself and other people.

5. Prioritize human interaction. Resist the urge to pick up your phone when you're interacting with someone in person. Save your social media consumption for times when you're alone.

6. Refrain from using a 15-minute social media session as a crutch for handling unwanted feelings, like boredom or social anxiety. Using social media as a security blanket for uncomfortable situations is a way of avoiding or denying the problem, instead of accepting and dealing with it.

7. Be present as you engage. While reading people's posts, acknowledge any emotions, thoughts, and bodily sensations that arise. Why does some content make you angry or jealous? Why do some posts evoke joy or laughter? Observe your breathing.

8. Post and let go. When you post something, don't get attached to the possible outcomes and reactions of others. Resist the urge for external validation, and remember your inherent right to be loved for just being a human being, regardless of the judgment of others.

7 Habits to Value

TIME: 15 minutes
BEST FOR: Living a life worth living

Our values are the map and compass for the journey of life; they help us navigate challenges and bring us closer to ultimate joy. Knowing what's important to you and living a life that keeps you close to your values aligns with many of the principles of self-compassion, including self-awareness, self-kindness, and self-acceptance. This exercise will help you clarify your values so you can develop value-aligned daily habits.

Steps

1. Record this exercise in your journal or in a separate place. When you think about what's important to you, what comes to mind? Use the words in the list below as inspiration, and take about three minutes to come up with as many values as you can. Write from instinct; don't overthink it.

Possible values: Which of these are especially important to you?

Adventure	Family	Loyalty
Ambition	Friendships	Music
Authenticity	Fun	Nature
Balance	Growth	Peace
Bravery	Humor	Pleasure
Challenge	Justice	Respect
Compassion	Kindness	Self-Compassion
Creativity	Knowledge	Spirituality
Consciousness	Laughter	Stability
Curiosity	Learning	Success
Determination	Love	Wisdom

2. Use the following prompts, adapted from acceptance and commitment therapy (ACT) techniques, to brainstorm additional values:

   + Think of three people you admire. They can be people you know or famous figures; they can be living or dead. Write down the qualities that you admire about these people. Add these traits to your list of values.

   + Think about the following areas of your life. For each one, consider how you'd want to be known, the type of person you would like to be. Write down the values that are necessary to be that person in each domain: family relationships, friendships, career, leisure activities, hobbies, personal development, parenting, emotional health, physical health, spirituality.

3. Look over the list of values you've compiled and pick your top three. Then, write down a daily habit or habits that can bring you closer to your top three values. For example, if your top three values are peace, spirituality, and nature, you might decide to go in your backyard each morning to pray.

Clean Home,
Clean Mind

TIME: 15 minutes
BEST FOR: Mental clarity

Keeping a tidy home is a great way to be kind to yourself and create peace of mind. Implement these two habits in the name of self-compassion, with the bonus of maintaining an environment that you love and enjoy.

Steps

1. **Make your bed in the morning.** This habit is simple but powerful. Start your day by making your bed to set the tone of a clean, organized space and to create a sense of accomplishment the moment you get up. Admiral William H. McRaven, author of *Make Your Bed: Little Things that Can Change Your Life . . . and Maybe the World,* shares that starting your day with making your bed sets a catalyst of completing tasks for your day. It's also a special treat for you to come home to a bed that is made.

2. **Do a 15-minute speed clean in the evening.** This habit can be completed at the end of the day before going to bed. Rather than letting minor cleaning tasks pile up from one day to the next, develop the habit of doing a quick clean to close out each day. Here's how it works:

   ✦ Pick one room to focus on each night. Start by setting a timer for 15 minutes and set an intention to stop when time's up. Overdoing it may burn you out and inhibit you from keeping up this habit.

+ Living Room: Focus on making the room presentable, and don't get stuck on small details. Create separate piles for things that will need to be moved to another room or trashed, and take them away at the end of your 15 minutes.

+ Kitchen: Focus on major tasks like taking out the trash, clearing the dishes, and decluttering the counters. End by cleaning and drying your sink.

+ Bathroom: Organize products and wipe down the counters. End by doing a quick wipe of the sink, toilet, and shower.

+ Bedrooms: Put away any clothes and shoes; put clothes that need laundering in a hamper or basket. Remove objects that belong elsewhere, and focus on reducing visual clutter so the space feels peaceful.

Fun Time

TIME: 20 Minutes
BEST FOR: Increasing moments of pleasure

Making sure your life is filled with pleasure is an important act of self-compassion. Cultivating joy is not about the absence of negative emotions; instead, it should focus on creating positive experiences that bring you feelings of happiness and excitement. Use this mindfulness strategy to create a habit of engaging in pleasurable activities every day.

Steps

1. Find a comfortable place to sit and reflect. Have a pen and paper nearby.

2. Start by acknowledging your right to experience pleasure. Repeat this mantra in your head three times as you breathe deeply: "I deserve to experience pleasure and joy."

3. Take a few more deep breaths, then close your eyes.

4. Tune into what brings you joy. Think about all the things that make you smile. Reflect on activities make you happy. What do you like to do for fun? Recall all the moments you have felt bliss, and think about what you were doing in those moments. Are there any common themes?

5. Open your eyes and write down your realizations about the things that bring you joy.

6. Close your eyes once more. It's well-established that helping other people brings about intense feelings of joy. Reflect on ways that you can serve others that would make you happy. Can you use your talents or resources to do volunteer work or aid a friend who's in need?

7. Open your eyes and write down these ideas. Then close your eyes again.

8. Visualize the perfect vacation for yourself, whether it's a place you've been or somewhere you'd like to go. Imagine where you would be, what you would be doing, and who would be with you.

9. Open your eyes and note all the things that brought you joy on your mental vacation.

10. Now, look at your list of pleasurable activities and situations. Take 10 minutes to think about how you can incorporate these into your everyday life. How can you make having fun a habit? Set aside 30 minutes each day to engage in at least one of the pleasurable activities you identified during this exercise.

10 One Thing at a Time

TIME: 15 minutes
BEST FOR: Decreasing feelings of being overwhelmed

Many people believe that multitasking helps them get more done. However, multitasking decreases productivity and efficiency. Conversely, the experience of doing only one thing at a time will ease your feelings of being overwhelmed. The more you "single task," the more you'll learn how satisfying and calming it is to give your all to one task. This mindfulness technique will help you learn to do just that, with full awareness moment by moment.

Steps

1. Begin by picking a small task or project that you would like to complete. It should be something that you could reasonably expect to finish in 15 minutes, so you won't feel rushed or pressured. Your task could be one part of a larger project, as long as there's a clear end point.

2. Set aside a block of time in your schedule when you can work on this project uninterrupted. Arrange to have all necessary materials and equipment on hand before you begin.

3. When it's time to start, set a timer and put away all distractions. If you're working on a computer, close all browsers unless you need internet access for your task. Mute your phone and turn off all notifications.

4. Play some music that will help you focus.

5. Start by using two minutes to tune into the present moment. Sit up tall in your work chair. Notice your surroundings. Breathe deeply and pay attention to what you see in the room: your desk, office supplies, the scene outside any nearby windows. Notice what you feel in your body as you sit supported by your chair, with your feet flat on the floor. Pay attention to any smells, such as your morning coffee or tea. Mindfully listen to your focus music. Use all your senses as you sit in stillness and take in the moment.

6. After two minutes of tuning into the present moment, begin working. Engage in the task with full awareness, and do not attach to any distractions that arise. Simply acknowledge distractions, such as thoughts or urges to multitask, by saying "I am distracted by _____. Now I will refocus on the task at hand."

7. When your timer sounds, take two additional minutes of stillness to notice how it feels to work on one thing at time.

11 Creative Juices

TIME: 20 minutes
BEST FOR: Reducing stress and anxiety

Much research has shown that creativity reduces stress and anxiety. Doing something creative is a great way to tap into all the principles of self-compassion, especially self-awareness, self-acceptance, patience, and perseverance. Use this mindfulness strategy to develop a habit of doing something creative daily.

Steps

1. **Schedule it.** Start by setting aside time in your calendar to be creative each day. Although it may seem counterintuitive to schedule creativity, having the time blocked out will help you to commit to it.

2. **Follow your natural interests.** You'll find some suggestions at the end of this exercise, but it's important that you engage in activities that align with your interests. Consider what you like to do, and what will build upon your authentic inclinations and strengths.

3. **Be open to the outcome.** Keep in mind that this creativity time is in the name of self-compassion. You should enjoy this time based on how you feel as you create. Do not get stuck evaluating the merits of your creations, but instead tune into the calm, focused feeling that comes with being creative.

4. **Go with the flow.** As you create, tune into your intuition and resist urges to be overly analytical with your creative process. Allow yourself to create freely. The more you do so, the easier it

will be to fall into a flow state, that sensation of being meditatively immersed in an activity.

5. **Be present.** Tuning into the present moment is a crucial factor in letting your creative juices flow. Use your senses: feel the materials you're working with, see the shapes and colors, hear the sounds. Check with your breathing as you create. If you notice shallow or rapid breaths, take a minute to breathe slowly and deeply.

6. **Keep it simple.** This brief creative time does not have to produce a complicated masterpiece. Anyone has the capacity to be creative. Here are some ideas to try:

+ Creating mandalas

+ Enjoying adult coloring books

+ Taking photographs

+ Writing short poems, reminiscences, or stories for fun

+ Scrapbooking

+ Blogging or vlogging

+ Making jewelry or working with clay

+ Cooking

+ Making music

+ Knitting

+ Working on an electronic or technology-based project

12 Be Here Now

TIME: 2 minutes
BEST FOR: Cultivating mindfulness throughout your day

Mindfulness isn't always about stepping away from daily life to sit and meditate. The great thing about mindfulness is it can be done anywhere, anytime. And the more you bring mindfulness into your life, the better you will be at consistently practicing compassion. Use this quick technique to reintroduce mindfulness throughout your day and, ultimately, to think more mindfully overall.

Steps

1. Set a reminder alarm on your phone to alert you to practice this two-minute exercise three times a day. If possible, set reminders for midmorning, midday, and midafternoon. Give the alarm a clear title that will inform you of your intention, such as "Be Here Now" or "Moment of Stillness."

2. When your reminder alerts you, stop what you're doing and take two minutes to be in the present moment. Make it a rule that you don't ignore this alert, and that you practice this quick and easy exercise whenever possible. Should you be involved with something urgent, delay the alarm by 30 minutes and practice the exercise as soon as possible.

3. Spend the first minute of the exercise engaging in balloon breathing: On your inhales, imagine sending air all the way to your belly, and expand your stomach as if it were a balloon filling up. Then slowly exhale, gradually deflating the balloon as your stomach muscles contract inward toward your spine. Be sure both your inhalations and exhalations are slow and controlled.

4. For the second minute, release control of your breath and breathe normally. Spend the second moment in stillness, observing the present moment. Take note of your surroundings, such as the people you're with and the environment you're in. Notice how you feel in the moment, both physically and emotionally. Observe any thoughts that run through your mind without attaching to them.

5. When the two minutes are up, thank yourself for taking the time to be present. Acknowledge how hard it is to stop in your tracks and be mindful. Feel a sense of pride for doing something good for yourself.

13 Break Time

TIME: 10 minutes

BEST FOR: Preventing and recovering from burnout

Burnout is a serious condition that we should do our best to prevent. This exercise will help you build the habit of regularly checking in with yourself to prevent burnout. It will teach you the warning signs and help you develop a plan to recover, should you suffer from this disorder.

Steps

1. First, mindfully set an intention to check in with yourself periodically (daily or weekly) and evaluate the possibility that you're experiencing burnout. During your check-ins, perform the following self-evaluation.

2. Start by looking for any of the following signs of burnout. Consider each symptom without judgment and decide if it applies to you.

   + Irritability

   + Feeling emotionally drained

   + Fatigue

   + Insomnia

   + Frequent headaches

   + Loss or increase of appetite

   + Decreased motivation

   + Increased anxiety

   + Feeling overwhelmed

+ Loss of pleasure in things that used to interest you

+ Apathy

+ Reduced job performance

+ Frequent upset stomach

+ Difficulty concentrating

3. Next, ask yourself the following questions:

+ Am I more cynical at work (or cynical about the work I do) than usual?

+ Am I less compassionate or patient than I used to be with coworkers, clients, and others I encounter during my day?

+ Do I find myself using alcohol or food on a regular basis to decompress from work?

+ Do I lack the energy to do anything during my leisure time?

4. Should you discover that you are in a state of burnout, implement a plan to recover. Here are some strategies to consider:

+ Remedy any changes or conditions that contributed to your burnout, such as overtime hours or poor boundaries with clients.

+ Accept that your plate is full. Say no to extra work and to those asking for favors, until you feel better.

+ Implement more breaks during your workday. Use the exercises in this book to give yourself periods of self-compassion, relaxation, and self-kindness.

+ Plan a vacation or take a leave of absence if necessary.

+ Increase your self-care. Eat healthier, exercise regularly, and get at least eight hours of sleep per night.

14 Night Night

TIME: 15 minutes
BEST FOR: Falling asleep easily

Deep, restful sleep is incredibly important for our mental and physical health! Giving yourself the gift of a good night's sleep rewards you in many ways: it can reduce stress, improve your memory, and decrease your risk of depression. With this meditative bedtime process, you can unwind at the end of each day and drift peacefully off to slumber.

Steps

1. First, start with a brief, simple, relaxing nighttime ritual: drinking a cup of hot chamomile tea, listening to relaxing music, or praying. (Bath Time Oasis, page 98, is a good prelude to this ritual if you have time.) This will become a signal to your brain that it's bedtime, for an easier time falling asleep.

2. Lie down on your bed in a comfortable position and close your eyes.

3. Focus your attention on relaxing your body. Working your way from your head down to your toes, imagine relaxing each part of your body, one by one.

4. Next, relax your whole body by imagining you are sinking into the bed. Feel all the tension leaving your body as you let go and your muscles melt down into the soft mattress.

5. As thoughts arise, say this mantra to yourself: "Tomorrow is a new day. I can think about this tomorrow. Right now, I deserve a good night's rest." Try your best not to get carried away by any one line of thought. If you do notice your mind is racing, note the theme of the thought, repeat the mantra, and thank yourself for noticing that your mind drifted away.

6. Without stressing about it, try to resist urges to move around, scratch, or fidget. Try to stay as still as possible and notice any bodily sensations without overly attaching to them. If you do need to move, do so gently and become still again.

7. Shift to focusing on your breath. Spend a few minutes inhaling deeply, filling your belly with air, and then slowly exhaling as your belly falls and you allow yourself to relax even more.

8. Let go of controlling your breath and simply observe your breathing until you drift off to sleep. Tune into your inhalations and feel your chest and belly rising. Notice if you naturally inhale through your mouth or through your nose. Pay attention to how your body relaxes as you exhale. Take note of the sound of your breathing.

REFLECTION ONE

In your journal, write down any current habits that are not aligned with self-compassion, such as smoking, working through lunch, rushing to work, sitting all day, too much screen time, and so on. Reflect on ways you can replace these habits with more self-compassionate practices.

REFLECTION TWO

Now that you're familiar with some long-term strategies after working through the exercises in this book, think about a day full of self-compassion. What would this day include, and what feelings might arise? Reflect on how you would savor good moments and how you would handle challenges on this day.

Final Thoughts

Congratulations on making it this far in your journey of mindful self-compassion! Though this is the end of the book, your experience with this practice is just beginning.

But first, you've been working hard, so take a moment to feel pride in how far you've come. You've learned to be more self-compassionate toward your thoughts, emotions, and body. You've become empowered to deal with judgmental thoughts, your inner critic, and difficult emotions such as shame and anxiety. You've also gained mindful self-compassion strategies to improve body positivity, self-care, and your overall physical health. Well done!

As you proceed, be gentle with yourself. Don't beat yourself up if you miss an exercise or aren't able to stick to your plan. Just keep at it. If you find yourself drifting away from your practice of mindful self-compassion, write in your journal about whatever has gotten in the way. Analyze the challenges you've listed, and brainstorm ways to overcome them. Write an intention to implement these solutions and remind yourself why. Write in detail about the reasons you decided to start practicing these exercises in the first place.

Remember that this journey isn't always a straight line. There will be moments when you detour from your goal of cultivating a more compassionate self. But as long as you find your way back and keep practicing, you can always access the tremendous benefits of mindful self-compassion. Remember that your objective is not to be perfect but to be kind.

Good luck! I wish you much happiness and self-love.

References

Birnie, Kathryn, Michael Speca, and Linda E. Carlson. "Exploring Self-Compassion and Empathy in the Context of Mindfulness-Based Stress Reduction (MBSR)." *Stress and Health* 26, no. 5 (November 29, 2010): 359–371. doi.org/10.1002 /smi.1305.

Blatt, S. J. "Representational Structures in Psychopathology." In *Rochester Symposium on Developmental Psychopathology: Emotion, Cognition, and Representation,* Vol. 6, edited by Dante Cicchetti and S. L. Toth (Rochester, NY: University of Rochester Press, 1995), 1–34.

Breines, Juliana G., and Serena Chen. "Self-Compassion Increases Self-Improvement Motivation." *Personality and Social Psychology Bulletin* 38, no. 9 (May 2012): 1133–1143. doi.org/10.1177/0146167212445599.

Brown, Brené. "Research." Accessed February 1, 2020. brenebrown.com /the-research.

Cuddy, Amy. "Your Body Language May Shape Who You Are." Filmed June 2012 at TEDGlobal. Video, 20:48. TED.com/talks/amy_cuddy_your_body_language_ may_shape_who_you_are?language=en.

Eisler, Melissa. "Laughter Meditation: 5 Healing Benefits and a 10-Minute Practice." The Chopra Center. Last modified March 27, 2017. chopra.com/articles /laughter-meditation-5-healing-benefits-and-a-10-minute-practice.

Field, Tiffany, Miguel Diego, Jeannette Delgado, Daniel Garcia, and C. G. Funk. "Hand Pain is Reduced by Massage Therapy." *Complementary Therapies in Clinical Practice* 17, no. 4 (November 2011): 226–229. doi.org/10.1016/j .ctcp.2011.02.006.

Gilbert, Paul. *Compassion Focused Therapy: Distinctive Features.* CBT Distinctive Features Series. (New York: Routledge, 2010).

Gilbert, Paul, and Chris Irons. "Focused Therapies and Compassionate Mind Training for Shame and Self-Attacking." In *Compassion: Conceptualisations, Research and Use in Psychotherapy,* edited by Paul Gilbert (London: Routledge, 2005), 263–325.

Hollis-Walker, Laurie, and Kenneth Colosimo. "Mindfulness, Self-Compassion, and Happiness in Non-Meditators: A Theoretical and Empirical Examination." *Personality and Individual Differences* 50, no. 2 (January 2011): 222–227. doi.org/10.1016/j.paid.2010.09.033.

Leary, Mark R., Eleanor B. Tate, Claire E. Adams, Ashley Batts Allen, and Jessica Hancock. "Self-Compassion and Reactions to Unpleasant Self-Relevant Events: The Implications of Treating Oneself Kindly." *Journal of Personality and Social Psychology* 92, no. 5 (2007): 887–904. self-compassion.org/wp-content /uploads/publications/LearyJPSP.pdf.

Neff, Kristin D. "Development and Validation of a Scale to Measure Self-Compassion." *Self and Identity* 2 (2003): 223–250. self-compassion.org /wp-content/uploads/publications/empirical.article.pdf.

———. "Self-Compassion: An Alternative Conceptualization of a Healthy Attitude Toward Oneself." *Self and Identity* 2 (2003): 85–101. doi.org /10.1080/15298860309032.

Neff, Kristin, and Christopher Germer. *The Mindful Self-Compassion Workbook: A Proven Way to Accept Yourself, Build Inner Strength, and Thrive.* New York: Guilford Press, 2018.

Neff, Kristin D., Ya-Ping Hsieh, and Kullaya Dejitthirat. "Self-Compassion, Achievement Goals, and Coping with Academic Failure." *Self and Identity* 4 (2005): 263–287. doi.org/10.1080/13576500444000317.

Neff, Kristin D., Kristin L. Kirkpatrick, and Stephanie S. Rude. "Self-Compassion and Adaptive Psychological Functioning." *Journal of Research in Personality* 41, no. 1 (February 2007): 139–154. doi.org/10.1016/j.jrp.2006.03.004.

Raes, Filip. "Rumination and Worry as Mediators of the Relationship between Self-Compassion and Depression and Anxiety." *Personality and Individual Differences* 48, no. 6 (April 2010): 757–761. doi.org/10.1016/j.paid.2010.01.023.

Wong, Cathy. "The Benefits of Progressive Muscle Relaxation." Last modified February 3, 2020. verywellmind.com/the-benefits-of-progressive-muscle -relaxation-90014.

Resources

Guided Meditations

Meditation Album by Tiffany Shelton Mariolle available at TiffanyShelton.com

Guided Meditations for concentration available on the Insight Timer app available at InsightTimer.com

Guided Meditations for Self-Compassion: Self-Compassion.org/category/exercises/#guided-meditations

Websites and Apps

Center for Mindful Self-Compassion: CenterForMSC.org

PomoDone App, Pomodoro Method app available at PomoDoneApp.com

Mindful Browsing, gentle reminders when you visit time-wasting sites: MindfulBrowsing.org

TED Talk on Power Poses: TED.com/talks/amy_cuddy_your_body_language_may_shape_who_you_are?language=en

Books

The Happiness Trap: How to Stop Struggling and Start Living; A Guide to ACT, by Dr. Russ Harris

Hardwiring Happiness, by Dr. Rick Hanson

Index

Guilt and shame (*continued*
  self-acceptance without shame, 4
  Shame Buster exercise, 90–91
  social media overuse as generating, 134
  Take the Leap activity for
    releasing, 24–25

H

Habits
  burnout, avoiding, 148–149
  compassionate thinking as a
    healthy habit, 66, 123
  creative activities, daily
    engagement in, 144–145
  empathy and understanding as
    a habitual response, 4
  fun time, daily scheduling of, 140–41
  home cleaning habits, 138–139
  mindfulness, breaking bad
    habits with, 1, 11, 88
  negative self-talk, breaking
    the habit of, 26, 32
  new routines, making habitual, 122
  reflection exercise, 152
  self-appreciation, getting
    into the habit of, 45
  social media habits, 134–135
  value-aligned daily habits,
    cultivating, 136–137
Hanson, Rick, 20, 44
Happiness and joy
  affirmations acknowledging, 25
  Daily Compassion Check-In
    as generating, 66
  Fun Time exercise to cultivate
    happiness, 140–141
  gratitude, daily happiness
    derived from, 9
  Me First exercise, happiness
    mantra used in, 82

mindfulness, happiness made
  possible through, 7, 10
patience, allowing for joy
  along the way, 5
as a personal value, 59
pleasure and joy, list of exercises
  to cultivate, 15
rewiring the brain to experience joy, 21
self-compassion leading to
  increase in, 2, 13
Taking in Your Good exercise
  to increase joy, 44–45
Hayes, Steven, 58
Hopelessness, counteracting,
  72–73, 74–75

I

Impatience. *See* Patience and perseverance
Inner critic and negativity
  critical self-talk examples, 66–67
  emotional suffering, managing
    responses to, 54–55
  Good Enough Mom visualization
    to dispel, 34–35
  inner bestie, creating to counteract, 85
  intrusive thoughts, 16, 28–29
  list of exercises for handling, 16
  negative core beliefs, unmasking,
    50–51
  negative self-talk, eliminating, 4, 13, 70
  negative thoughts, capturing
    when they occur, 26
  negativity bias, 20, 21, 44
  One-Two-Three Break for relief, 64–65
  Peace in a Box, soothing negative
    emotions via, 78–79
  Roster of Kindness activity
    to dispel, 32–33
  See also Self-criticism and self-judgment

Acknowledgments

First and foremost I would like to thank my incredible husband, daughter, and mother for filling my life with compassion. I am also grateful for my incredible friends and family, who have shown me grace and support. I want to offer my sincere gratitude for the editors that have helped make this book incredible, especially Lori Tenny and Rick Chillot. I want to thank Callisto Media for trusting me to write a book that I hope will help many people. I am grateful to the self-compassion experts that have inspired me along my own self-compassion journey and expertise, including Tara Brach and Dr. Kristin Neff. Also, I would like to acknowledge my psychology mentors that have guided me along a path to learn the psychological tools to help so many, including but not limited to Dr. Lynn Northrop and Dr. Peter Theodore. Finally, I want to acknowledge the readers of this book for investing in their well-being and trusting me to guide them.

About the Author

TIFFANY SHELTON MARIOLLE, PhD, is a psychologist, author, and entrepreneur helping people find peace of mind, brain, and spirit. She combines her expertise in psychology, neuropsychology, meditation, and entrepreneurship to help people cope with life's stressors and go from overwhelmed by life to thriving in life. Her mission is to help folks take care of their mental, brain, and spiritual health. Dr. Shelton Mariolle fulfills this mission with meditation albums, writings, online content, teaching, research, and psychological services.

CPSIA information can be obtained
at www.ICGtesting.com
Printed in the USA
JSHW040808020720
6447JS00005B/50